W9-ADL-614

SINATRA
HOLLYWOOD
HIS WAY

SINATRA

HOLLYWOOD HIS WAY

TIMOTHY KNIGHT

RUNNING PRESS
PHILADELPHIA · LONDON

9   8   7   6   5   4   3   2   1

Digit on the right indicates the number of this printing

Library of Congress Control Number: 2009942072

ISBN 978-0-7624-3743-6

Designed by Jason Kayser

Edited by Cindy De La Hoz

Typography: Bembo, Gotham, Knockout, and Ziggurat

Running Press Book Publishers

2300 Chestnut Street

Philadelphia, PA 19103-4371

Visit us on the web!

www.runningpress.com

Photo Credits

Photo on cover: © Michael Ochs Archive/Getty Images

Photos on pages 41–42, 75–76, 109, 111, 133 (left), 135, 151–153,
237, 239–240, 281 (left), 282–283, 285–287, 309, 311:
Courtesy of Everett Collection

Photos on pages 133 (right) and 281 (right):
Courtesy of CSU Archives/Everett Collection

To Les Krantz, my longtime mentor and good friend

CONTENTS

11	Introduction
13	Part 1: Frankie's Rise and Fall, 1941–1952
16	Higher and Higher
20	Step Lively
28	Anchors Aweigh
36	It Happened in Brooklyn
40	The Miracle of the Bells
44	The Kissing Bandit
48	Take Me Out to the Ball Game
58	On the Town
66	Double Dynamite
74	Meet Danny Wilson
79	Other Sinatra Films, 1941–1952

83	Part 2: The Crooner Comes Back, 1953–1959
86	From Here to Eternity
94	Suddenly
100	Young at Heart
108	Not as a Stranger
112	Guys and Dolls
118	The Tender Trap
124	The Man with the Golden Arm
132	Johnny Concho
136	High Society
144	The Pride and the Passion
150	The Joker Is Wild
154	Pal Joey
162	Kings Go Forth
168	Some Came Running
174	A Hole in the Head
180	Never So Few
189	Other Sinatra Films, 1953–1959

191	Part 3: The Rat Pack Years, 1960–1964
194	Can-Can
202	Ocean's Eleven
212	The Devil at 4 O'Clock
220	Sergeants 3
228	The Manchurian Candidate
236	Come Blow Your Horn
242	4 for Texas
246	Robin and the Seven Hoods
255	Other Sinatra Films, 1960–1964

259 | Part 4: Sinatra's Hollywood Twilight, 1965–1991

262 | None But the Brave

270 | Von Ryan's Express

276 | Marriage on the Rocks

280 | Assault on a Queen

284 | The Naked Runner

288 | Tony Rome

294 | The Detective

302 | Lady in Cement

308 | Dirty Dingus Magee

312 | The First Deadly Sin

319 | Other Sinatra Films, 1965–1991

323 | Bibliography

326 | Index

336 | Acknowledgements

Frankie and Frankie, a legend in the making in the early 1940s.

INTRODUCTION

IN THE SCORES of posthumous tributes paid Frank Sinatra after his death in 1998, most focused on his extraordinary reign as "The Voice" of twentieth-century pop music. No other singer had ever transfixed so many for so long, in a decades-spanning career that flourished for nearly sixty years and numbered close to 2,000 recordings. The late Elvis Presley may have been "The King," but for millions of fans around the world, Sinatra occupied a position even more rarefied than pop-star royalty. In their eyes, the high-school dropout from a working class Hoboken, New Jersey family was simply the "Chairman of the Board." But Sinatra was much more than a pop-music icon or Italian-American success story.

He was also a bona-fide movie star, a magnetic actor whom critic David Thomson described as ". . . a noir sound, like saxophones, foghorns, gunfire, and the quiet weeping of women in the background." Yet despite sixty-odd movies, an Academy Award, and five straight years as a top ten box-office draw, Sinatra never quite got his due in the Hollywood pantheon. He is considered a singer first—an actor second. Yet with the possible exception of his idol Bing Crosby, no other singer has ever enjoyed more lasting crossover success on the big screen than Sinatra. Or courted public rejection by tackling challenging, image-busting roles in provocative films. Just try to imagine either Presley or Crosby stepping into Sinatra's role as a would-be presidential

assassin in *Suddenly* (1954). It's doubtful that audiences would buy either of them as the paranoid war veteran holding a family hostage, whereas Sinatra is eerily persuasive in the role. He would push himself even further the following year, when he gave an astonishing, Oscar-nominated performance as a drug addict struggling to kick the habit in *The Man with the Golden Arm* (1955). While Otto Preminger's film may strike contemporary viewers as a hopelessly dated melodrama, Sinatra's performance holds up beautifully.

Admittedly, Sinatra made his share of duds. (What star hasn't?) And in a few films, he appears to be going through the motions, as if he's too bored by the material to care. But at his very best in films—*From Here to Eternity* (1953), *The Manchurian Candidate* (1962), and *Pal Joey* (1957), to name three—Sinatra brings an electric, jazzy energy to the screen. Whether he's singing and dancing with Gene Kelly in *On the Town* (1949) or trading wisecracks between martinis with his Rat Pack buddies in *Ocean's Eleven* (1960), Sinatra has charisma to burn. He effortlessly passes the Hollywood litmus test of true stardom: You can't take your eyes off him.

From fluffy romantic comedies to hard-hitting dramas to nail-biting thrillers, Sinatra covered the genre waterfront during his forty-one-year film career. *Sinatra: Hollywood His Way* is a celebration of the very best of "Ol' Blue Eyes" on the big screen.

young Frank Sinatra of MGM d

PART 1

FRANKIE'S RISE AND FALL

1941–1952

T HE 1940s would see both the zenith and nadir of Frank Sinatra's career. His rise to stardom and subsequent fall from grace seemed to mirror the crooner's own somewhat Jekyll-and-Hyde persona. The success of the newly crowned "Sultan of Swoon" was born of his own ambition, his ability to learn from the right mentors, and that elusive lady luck. From early on, Sinatra knew

he would need to attract the attention of the big-band leaders if he was going to attract any recording industry or public attention at all. In 1940, he did just that, signing with the Tommy Dorsey Orchestra. It proved to be a fruitful and fortuitous partnership with Dorsey that lasted, officially, two years.

Sinatra, who never had formal training as a singer or performer and could not read music, studied both Dorsey's musical phrasing and his showmanship, with spectacular results. Bobbysoxers were soon screaming and swooning before Sinatra could even step out from behind the curtains. He poured his soul into every

performance and sang with a confidence that belied his relative inexperience. As his popularity skyrocketed, Sinatra became one of the first big-band vocalists to close a live show—and he received more applause than the band.

The Tommy Dorsey Orchestra also provided Sinatra's entrée to Hollywood after Paramount Pictures hired the band to appear in *Las Vegas Nights* (1941), an admittedly run-of-the-mill musical comedy. Sinatra earned his first, albeit uncredited, screen time as a featured vocalist performing "I'll Never Smile Again" with the singing group the Pied Pipers. He next performed a few songs in the MGM musical *Ship Ahoy* (1942), a bit of wartime fluff starring Eleanor Powell and Red Skelton.

Between 1940 and 1943, Sinatra was listed as *Down Beat* magazine's top musical performer, knocking Bing Crosby out of the coveted position. In 1942, Sinatra's appearance at New York's Paramount Theater gave proof of growing "Sinatramania," as fans screamed their adoration and he was deemed the "hottest thing in showbiz." His appeal crossed multiple social and gender lines. As few male performers could, he drew admiration from men as well as women; from adults; tweens; and of course, the growing teen population.

Although Sinatra had married his longtime sweetheart Nancy Barbato in 1939, he nevertheless indulged in a series of affairs that reportedly embarrassed his wife, the mother of his three children: Nancy, Frank Jr., and Tina. And as his star rose, Sinatra also became increasingly volatile and temperamental. He often fired back at the conservative press, who criticized him for failing to serve in the war (he was classified 4-F) and for his outspoken support of President Franklin Roosevelt. Such hotheaded tendencies led to Sinatra's arrest in 1947, when he punched New York columnist Lee Mortimer for suggesting that the crooner had Mafia ties.

Nor did Sinatra win any friends in Hollywood when he voiced his frustration with the filmmaking process, saying, "Pictures stink." Impatient with doing multiple takes, he often refused to do more than one take for a shot, fearful his performance would lose spontaneity. Ironically, he would find some of his greatest success in a series of three musicals with hoofer Gene Kelly, known for his rigorous and demanding dance rehearsals. Kelly wisely tailored routines to Sinatra's natural grace, if limited athletic ability. Their pairing helped create some of the most memorable and iconic moments in film.

But as Sinatra's popularity declined, due to shifting musical tastes and increasing media criticism, the crooner became desperate to salvage his film career. He took roles in forgettable, critically panned box-office bombs, such as *The Kissing Bandit* (1948), which only hastened his fall from commercial grace.

The dissolution of Sinatra's marriage, instigated by his affair with Ava Gardner, didn't help matters. The two seemed magnetically drawn by their mutual passion, temper, and neuroses, but she refused to continue the relationship unless he divorced Nancy. By 1951, her wish was granted, and Sinatra and Gardner were finally married.

But by 1951, Sinatra would find himself confronting greater threats to his career. The Red Scare spread and the House Un-American Activities Committee began rounding up suspected communists in Hollywood. Sinatra would find himself having to defend his family's and his own liberal tendencies, though he was never brought before the committee.

By 1952, attendance at his live performances had waned, his days at Columbia Records were numbered, and his agency, MCA, informed him they would no longer represent him. Within little more than a decade, Sinatra, now in his late thirties, found himself a "has-been."

Right: Frank Sinatra sheet music; the crooner would soon turn movie star.

Below: Frank Sinatra was a hit in a trio of films with Gene Kelly in the mid to late '40s. Here they perform in *Take Me Out to the Ball Game*.

HIGHER AND HIGHER

AN RKO-RADIO PICTURE | 1943

Director
Tim Whelan

Screenplay
Jay Dratler and Ralph Spence

Based on the musical by Gladys
Hurlbut and Joshua Logan

Principal Cast
Frank Sinatra (as himself),
Michèle Morgan (Millie Pico),
Jack Haley (Mike O'Brien), Leon
Errol (Cyrus Drake), Marcy
McGuire (Mickey), Victor Borge
(Sir Victor Fitzroy Victor), Mary
Wickes (Sandy Brooks), Elisabeth
Risdon (Mrs. Georgia Keating),
Barbara Hale (Katherine
Keating), Mel Tormé (Marty), Paul
Hartman (Byngham), Grace
Hartman (Hilda), Dooley Wilson
(Oscar), Ivy Scott (Mrs. Whiffin)

"**GOOD MORNING,** my name is Frank Sinatra." With those seven words, Sinatra launched a movie career that would span decades. *Higher and Higher* wasn't Sinatra's first film; he'd previously done musical cameos in a few others, but this RKO film gave him his first starring role.

Then in his late twenties and rail thin, Sinatra was already America's first teen music idol when RKO signed him to a seven-year contract (later bought out by MGM) and cast him in *Higher and Higher* at the last minute. He plays the singing, piano-playing neighbor of Cyrus Drake (Leon Errol), a down-and-out millionaire who passes his scullery maid Millie (French star Michèle Morgan) off as his long-lost daughter in hopes of marrying her off into wealth. It takes nearly a half hour of the ninety-minute film for Sinatra to appear—but when he does, he rescues this adaptation of a 1940 Broadway musical from mediocrity.

When RKO executives bought the script to the Broadway show, they somehow neglected to purchase the rights to *Higher and Higher*'s chief selling point: a great score by Richard Rodgers and Lorenz Hart. RKO instead hired Jimmy McHugh and Harold Donaldson to write new songs for Sinatra, which he performs with a show stopping display of his dazzlingly versatile voice: "This is a Lovely Way to Spend an Evening," "The Music Stopped," and "I Couldn't Sleep a Wink Last Night." The last was

Left: Sinatra, Mickey (Marcy McGuire), and Marty (Mel Tormé) ham it up at Drake's nightclub.

Right: Sinatra finds himself falling in love with Millie (Michéle Morgan), the scullery maid posing as an heiress.

nominated for an Academy Award, as was Constantin Bakaleinikoff's score. Though neither won, *Higher and Higher* had no trouble attracting business. "Wink" and "Evening" went on to become big hits for the crooner, and presumably the film itself was just what war-weary audiences needed—lighthearted escapism.

Of course, for Sinatra, comparisons with Bing Crosby were inevitable; in fact, a line in the film jokingly makes the connection. Crosby had launched his own Hollywood career playing himself in Paramount's *The Big Broadcast* (1929), and was scheduled for a cameo in *Higher and Higher,* though it never materialized. Thirteen years would pass before Sinatra and Crosby finally shared the screen in *High Society* (1956).

While no one mistook *Higher and Higher* for great art, most critics saw Sinatra's screen potential, with the possible exception of the curmudgeonly Bosley Crowther of the *New York Times.* Crowther, who would go on to have a love/hate critic's relationship with Sinatra, sarcastically renamed the film *Lower and Lower* and said, "Frankie is no Gable or Barrymore and the movie registers as a slapdash setting for the incredibly unctuous renderings of the Voice." But Crowther was in the distinct minority, as critics and film-goers eagerly welcomed a new singing superstar into the Hollywood fold.

Opposite: Sinatra and Millie look on while Oscar (Dooley Wilson) plays piano at the Drake Mansion.

Above: Sinatra is literally on cloud nine at the conclusion of *Higher and Higher*.

STEP LIVELY

AN RKO-RADIO PICTURE | 1944

Director
Tim Whelan

Screenplay
Warren Duff and Peter Milne

Based on the play *Room Service*
by Allen Boretz and John Murray

Principal Cast
Frank Sinatra (Glenn Russell),
George Murphy (Gordon Miller),
Gloria DeHaven (Christine
Marlowe), Adolphe Menjou
(Wagner), Eugene Pallette
(Jenkins), Walter Slezak (Joe
Gribble), Wally Brown (Binion)

IN LATER YEARS, Frank Sinatra would accumulate the nicknames "Ol' Blue Eyes" and "Chairman of the Board," sobriquets befitting a world weary, sophisticated star. But just twenty-eight in 1944, he was still the skinny kid from Hoboken, the idol of bobbysoxers. He had three movies under his belt, but he was merely the uncredited singer in Tommy Dorsey's band in the first two, *Las Vegas Nights* (1941) and *Ship Ahoy* (1942). In the third, *Higher and Higher* (1943), he got the chance to try his hand at acting, although playing himself was not much of a stretch. It wasn't until 1944 that Hollywood fully unleashed "The Voice" on the movies with a starring role in the musical comedy, *Step Lively*. If Sinatra's amiable performance does not fully take advantage of his performing skills as *Anchors Aweigh* (1945) would the next year, or hint at the emotional depths he would achieve in his Oscar-winning turn in *From Here to Eternity* (1953), it at least suggests that his talents were not simply limited to a velvet voice and the ability to make women swoon.

Sinatra plays Glenn Russell, a sweetly naïve playwright who is swept into scheming Broadway director Gordon Miller's (George Murphy) chaotic universe. The director and his entire company have set up shop in a chic Manhattan hotel, running up huge bills as they rehearse their new musical in Miller's suite, and keeping one step ahead

"That guy is the greatest discovery of my career. Did you see the women around the room while he was singing? Did you see the expressions on their faces? If that guy was the Pied Piper of Hamelin, there wouldn't be a dame left in town."

Gordon Miller (George Murphy) defining playwright Glenn Russell's (Sinatra) true talent

"I didn't learn. I just sang, I guess."

Russell answering the question, "Where did you learn to sing like that?"

Left: The young Frank Sinatra strikes a pose that will become a familiar sight in the coming decades.

Right: Mistaking playwright Glenn Russell for a potential backer, Gordon fetes him with alcohol and a cigar.

of Wagner (Adolphe Menjou), the hotel boss who is trying to evict them. Russell mistakenly believes the troupe is putting on his socially conscious play and Miller is anxious to be rid of him. But when he hears Russell sing, he realizes he has found a new star—that is, if he ever gets a chance to mount the show.

This was the second adaptation of Allen Boretz and John Murray's 1937 Broadway smash *Room Service*. The play was refashioned as a Marx Brothers vehicle in 1938, a marriage of slapstick farce with zany comedians that did not quite gel. Frank S. Nugent, critic for the *New York Times* observed, "There was nothing subtle in the [play's] writing; slapstick seldom is; but on the stage it had the advantage of seeming possible. The producing trio did the most incredible things, but did them out of desperation. With the Marx Brothers, absurdities seem always to be wooed for their own sake. That's a weakness of the picture." Filmgoers evidently agreed. RKO paid $255,000 for the screen rights. The movie went on to lose more than $300,000.

Anxious to see some return on its investment, the studio sought a foolproof box-office draw for the remake, creating an opportunity for Sinatra. After steadily making a name for himself as a singer, first with Harry James and then with Tommy Dorsey's band, he hit the showbiz stratosphere as a solo act when he opened for Benny Goodman at New York's Paramount Theater during an engagement that began on New Year's Eve 1942. The show transformed Sinatra into a genuine phenomenon: the first teen idol of America. His popularity among the bobbysoxer set promised a built-in audience for *Step Lively*. At the same time, the musical's screwball humor and romance offered appeal beyond Sinatra's young constituency; it gave the singer the chance to broaden his own fan base. This was a win-win situation for both studio and star.

In addition to providing Sinatra with his first real acting job and giving him his first top billing, there were other firsts involved with the making of *Step Lively*. Although he would not truly show how well he could move until his three musicals with Gene Kelly—*Anchors Aweigh, Take Me Out to the Ball Game* (1949), and *On the Town* (1949)—under the

Opposite top: Chorus girls surround bathing beauty Christine (Gloria DeHaven) as she luxuriates in the bubbles.

Opposite bottom: Gordon Miller (George Murphy), Christine Marlowe (Gloria DeHaven), and the chorus rehearse in Gordon's suite.

Below: Christine and Glenn share a cab and a smooch.

"He's got charm and personality and that voice! Ho ho!"

Miller singing Russell's praises

Below: Glenn and Christine make beautiful music together.

Opposite top: Christine and Glenn's number ends in a big finish.

Opposite bottom: Christine and Glenn lead the chorus as they trip the light fantastic.

tutelage of *Step Lively* choreographer Ernst Matray, Sinatra proved himself no slouch as a dancer, holding his own in a cast that included ace hoofer George Murphy. The movie also afforded Sinatra his first screen kiss, a chaste smooch with love interest Gloria DeHaven, an occasion of such importance that *Look* magazine devoted a lavish, four-page spread to it. More important to Sinatra's future were the contributions of songwriters Sammy Cahn and Jule Styne. The tunesmiths were still in the early days of a partnership that began in 1942, and though this nascent collaboration did not yield any terrifically memorable songs, it signaled the beginning of a fruitful relationship with Sinatra.

Upon *Step Lively*'s July 1944 release, *Time* magazine predicted, "Sinatra's name on the marquee is sufficient to guarantee lipsticky posters on the outside, moaning galleryites within." The movie was indeed a hit with his fans. The critics were mostly indifferent to it, but many had kind words for the star. "*Step Lively* is not a very good dish for Sinatra, although it demonstrates that he has far more performing range and assurance than

many might have suspected," wrote Howard Barnes in the *New York Herald Tribune*. Archer Winston in the *New York Post* was equally complimentary, declaring, "Sinatra . . . is better than in his previous movie efforts. He looks better, acts better, and sings in the manner that has made him famous. If it were not for the rampant demonstration of his fanatics, there would be little to hold against him."

A dissenter was the *New York Times*' Bosley Crowther. In general, it is a positive review, as he concludes, "The whole film was rigged up to ride [Sinatra]. And it carries his meager weight quite well." However, when Crowther writes, "as the yokel playwright who now can sing (a matter, that is, of opinion)," his disdain for one of the greatest vocal talents of the twentieth century is evident. The fans paid Crowther no mind and Sinatra got the last laugh, as *Step Lively* was but the first lively step in the singer's rapid rise to full-fledged movie stardom.

Above: A playwright no more, Glenn finds his home in the spotlight and a star is born.

Opposite: While Gordon looks on, Glenn and Christine celebrate their blooming relationship.

ANCHORS AWEIGH

AN MGM PICTURE | 1945

Director
George Sidney

Screenplay
Isobel Lennart

Principal Cast
Frank Sinatra (Clarence Doolittle), Kathryn Grayson (Susan Abbott), Gene Kelly (Joe Brady), José Iturbi (himself), Dean Stockwell (Donald Martin), Pamela Britton (waitress from Brooklyn), Grady Sutton (Bertram Kraler), Sharon McManus (little girl beggar)

FOR ANYONE who hadn't yet noticed the skinny crooner from Hoboken, the "Columbus Day riots" of October 1944 sent a message that was heard around the world. For hoards of excited fans, New York City's Paramount Theater became the center of the universe when Frank Sinatra performed for thousands inside, while tens of thousands outside filled the streets. Hundreds of police officers rushed in, trying to make sense and order out of the chaos inspired by the music idol.

Hollywood rushed in too, with MGM offering Sinatra a multiyear contract, and a chance to make Technicolor movie musicals at the studio that invented the style. In a matter of months, the studio's musical production unit was ready to start work on Sinatra's first big-budget film spectacle, *Anchors Aweigh* (1945). The studio created a perfect package for Sinatra, with top billing, songs by hit makers Sammy Cahn and Jule Styne, multi-talented co-stars, and a clever storyline that emphasized the tender, sentimental side of Sinatra so familiar to fans of his records and radio performances.

As the meek-mannered Clarence Doolittle, a sailor on leave with a wide-eyed "gee whiz" demeanor, Sinatra plays the innocent in *Anchors Aweigh* with Gene Kelly as his rakish mentor, Joe Brady, the notorious "Sea Wolf" reputed to have a girl in every port. When the pair earns four

> "I've been in the Navy a year and a half now. Every time we hit port and get liberty, all I do is go to the library."

Clarence Doolittle (Sinatra) to Joseph Brady (Gene Kelly)

> "Let me see a sample of your technique. You're you, see, and I'm a dame coming down the street. Pick me up."

Joe Brady to Clarence Doolittle

Left: Clarence and Joe celebrate a four-day shore leave with a song.

Right: Long before his fame as an adult, Dean Stockwell played a young wannabe sailor opposite Sinatra in *Anchors Aweigh*.

Above: Sinatra put in months of intense training to perfect his dance routines with Gene Kelly in *Anchors Aweigh*. Kelly choreographed all of the film's dance sequences.

Opposite: Clarence listens in as Joe lines up a date for shore leave.

days leave in Los Angeles, Clarence tags along with Joe to learn how it's done, and gets a crash course on the art of the pick-up. Before they can get started, however, they're further waylaid by a young runaway named Donnie (Dean Stockwell), whom they escort home to his guardian aunt, a struggling singer named Susan (Kathryn Grayson) who instantly becomes the object of Clarence's affection.

Although Joe considers "Aunt Susie" to be a waste of time, he's soon embroiled in an elaborate scheme to secure her an audition with the famous motion picture music director José Iturbi (as himself); once Joe hears her sing, he's instantly smitten with her. Just as suddenly, Clarence realizes that the real love of his life is not Susan but a waitress he calls "Brooklyn" (Pamela Britton), whose East Coast accent, to Clarence's delight, is even thicker than his. Before the romances can be realigned, there are plenty of opportunities for song and dance, including Sinatra's sublime versions of "I Fall in Love Too Easily" and "What Makes the Sun Set?"; the sailors' duet "We Hate to Leave"; and the many astounding Kelly-Sinatra dance sequences in which the world's greatest

"I didn't save your life to hand it over to that character. I'm gonna get you a dame that's a dame."

Joe Brady to Clarence Doolittle

singer tries to keep up with the world's greatest dancer—and mostly succeeds. The musical numbers stand on their own, which is fortunate since they often have little or nothing to do with the central story. Case in point: the iconic number pairing Kelly with the cartoon mouse Jerry of *Tom and Jerry*.

Sinatra took the filmmaking process seriously, and worked hard to give his best in *Anchors Aweigh*. He admired Gene Kelly immensely, and was grateful for the chance to learn about movies from a master; in later years he credited Kelly with teaching him the essentials of the profession and giving him the confidence he felt he lacked at the start. For many of the musical numbers in *Anchors Aweigh*, Sinatra needed to dance the same steps as Kelly. To reach that level of finesse he practiced six days a week for two months before shooting at MGM studios began. He only danced passably, Sinatra said, because Kelly had simplified the routines for him. He also credited Kelly with teaching him the patience needed for a production of this complexity, in which certain scenes had to be shot dozens of times over the course of days or even weeks.

Although the press had promoted Sinatra eagerly in the first years of his fame, he discovered during the making of *Anchors Aweigh* that they could easily turn against him if the story was right. During a break from filming, Sinatra vented to a reporter about the industry, and quotes from the interview—later denied by Sinatra—were widely circulated, such as, "Pictures stink. Most of the people in them do, too." Sinatra issued a response and the matter faded quickly, but it was a turning point in his relationship with the press. Up to then, the media had been reliable advocates, ignoring missteps and eagerly publishing exaggerated versions of the Sinatra Effect, such as the delirium of the bobbysoxers who screamed ceaselessly at Sinatra concerts and delivered practiced swoons.

Publicity stunts aside, enthusiasm for all things Sinatra was real, and a whiff of negative press had no apparent effect on the Sinatra phenomenon, as evidenced by the crowds who packed movie theaters when *Anchors Aweigh* opened in July 1945, making it one of the biggest

Top: *Anchors Aweigh* was the first of three MGM musicals starring Sinatra and Kelly.

Center: Joe dances with Jerry the mouse in the film's classic fantasy sequence.

Bottom: While waiting for her big break, Susan (Kathryn Grayson) sings in a local restaurant.

Opposite: Clarence joins famed music director José Iturbu for an impromptu duet.

hits of the year. "All the world knows Frank Sinatra can sing. Now it turns out he can act, too" Thalia Bell wrote in her review for *Motion Picture Herald*. And *Los Angeles Examiner* columnist Louella Parsons summed up the film by saying, "It has sock artists, sock tunes, and sock dances, all given by three stars who are tops in their individual lines." The film community also signaled their approval, giving the film Academy Award nominations for Best Picture, Best Actor for Gene Kelly, Best Original Song for "I Fall in Love Too Easily," and Best Color Cinematography, and awarding the statuette to George Stoll for Best Musical Score.

A cultural shift was underway, and this film was a catalyst. *Anchors Aweigh* drew Sinatra's young, excitable fans, but it also attracted an older audience who never would have stood in line all night just to hear him sing. For the first time, the full magnitude of his talent was on display for audiences everywhere, and his appeal onscreen would make him a truly cross-generational star. Now everyone could see what the screaming was all about: Sinatra could do it all.

"Look, I didn't ask you to save my life, but you did. So now I figure you're responsible for me."

Clarence Doolittle

IT HAPPENED IN BROOKLYN

AN MGM PICTURE | 1947

Director
Richard Whorf

Screenplay
Isobel Lennart

Story
J. P. McGowan

Principal Cast
Frank Sinatra (Danny Miller),
Kathryn Grayson (Anne
Fielding), Peter Lawford
(Jamie Shellgrove), Jimmy
Durante (Nick Lombardi),
Gloria Grahame (Nurse)

IT HAPPENED IN BROOKLYN is pleasant if forgettable, a featherweight musical with a shopworn plot, and yet it's a key film in Frank Sinatra's cinematic career. Two years before *On the Town* (1949) created a stir with its location shooting in New York, Sinatra stepped on the Brooklyn Bridge to sing a Sammy Cahn/Jule Styne ode to the New York landmark. It is also the film for which he recorded "Time After Time," a Cahn/Styne composition that was destined to become one of his classic tunes. Not only that, but his performance is so assured in this MGM film that critics took notice, acknowledging his growth as an actor.

Danny Miller (Sinatra) returns to civilian life in Brooklyn at the end of World War II dreaming of becoming a singer. After old buddy Nick Lombardi (Jimmy Durante) helps him conquer his stage fright, Danny forms a songwriting partnership with his visiting English musician pal Jamie Shellgrove (future Rat Pack member Peter Lawford). But success comes at a great cost for the aspiring singer, when Jamie falls for Danny's girlfriend, music teacher Anne Field (Kathryn Grayson).

It Happened in Brooklyn came at a difficult time for Sinatra. He wanted to marry his mistress, singer/actress Marilyn Maxwell, but his wife Nancy refused to divorce him. He took his unhappiness out on the production, frequently coming late to work and sometimes not showing up

"I suppose the biggest revelation of *It Happened in Brooklyn* . . . is the way Frank Sinatra seems to have loosened up and got into the swing of things as a film player and even as a comedian. Things look promising for Frankie boy in films, even if his wooing notes should one day peter out."

John McManus, *PM*

"Whenever I have to sing for strangers, I freeze up."

Danny Miller (Sinatra) confessing to stage fright

Left: A skeptical nurse (Gloria Grahame) challenges shy Danny Miller to come out of his shell.

Right: Three friends form a romantic triangle when Jamie Shellgrove (Peter Lawford) and Danny introduce Anne Fielding (Kathryn Grayson) to their song, "Time After Time."

Above: Returning soldier Danny celebrates his homecoming by paying a visit to his beloved Brooklyn Bridge.

Opposite: Danny and old pal Nick Lombardi (Jimmy Durante) nail his audition at the music store with a big finish.

at all. When comic Phil Silvers's partner, Rags Ragland, died suddenly, Sinatra stepped in to perform with Silvers at New York's Copacabana nightclub. It was a heartfelt gesture to a friend, but one that created more absences on the set, infuriating the studio. Despite the shenanigans, director Richard Whorf observed, "Directing Frank is a revelation. He blends in more than you'd think with the other cast members. He once said to me, 'When everyone else is in top form, they improve my form.' He believed in team work."

Though *It Happened in Brooklyn* received middling reviews, Sinatra's notices were glowing. "Frank, of course, thrills the customers with his vocalizing, but it's his naturalness and easygoing charm that beget applause. It just seems like all of the sudden it's spring and Frankie is an actor," wrote the *Los Angeles Examiner*'s Sara Hamilton, while *Variety* raved, "Guy's acquired the Bing Crosby knack of nonchalance, throwing away his gag lines with fine aplomb." Even *New York Times* critic Bosley Crowther had to admit, "Maybe you won't believe this (and it happens in Brooklyn, don't forget), but Mr. Sinatra turns in a performance of considerable casual charm. He acts with some ease and dexterity."

With *It Happened in Brooklyn*, Sinatra finally proved himself as an actor. Now he just needed quality material to showcase the full range of his talent onscreen.

THE MIRACLE OF THE BELLS

AN RKO-RADIO PICTURE | 1948

Director

Irving Pichel

Screenplay

Ben Hecht, Quentin Reynolds, and Dewitt Bodeen

Based on the novel by Russell Janney

Principal Cast

Fred MacMurray (William Dunnigan), Alida Valli (Olga Treskovna), Frank Sinatra (Father Paul), Lee J. Cobb (Marcus Harris), Harold Vermilyea (Nick Orloff), Charles Meredith (Father J. Spinsky), Jim Nolan (Tod Jones), Veronica Pataky (Anna Klovna), Philip Ahn (Ming Gow), Frank Ferguson (Dolan), Frank Wilcox (Dr. Jennings)

THE YEAR 1948 was *annus horribilis* for Sinatra's film career, which nosedived with the release of back-to-back flops, *The Miracle of the Bells* and *The Kissing Bandit.* He would briefly rebound from career oblivion the following year with *On the Town,* but the critical and commercial failure of these two films virtually rendered Sinatra persona non grata in Hollywood.

To say that *The Miracle of the Bells* is better than *The Kissing Bandit* is the essence of faint praise. Irving Pichel's turgid adaptation of Russell Janney's 1946 bestselling novel casts Sinatra in one of the most unlikely roles of his career: a sensitive Roman Catholic priest in a Pennsylvania coalmining town. Playing essentially a supporting role to Fred MacMurray and Italian actress Alida Valli—billed here simply as Valli—Sinatra took a drubbing from critics like *Time*'s reviewer, who described him as "looking rather fleabitten." Thirty-two years later, Harry and Michael Medved paid cheeky tribute to Sinatra's maligned performance in their 1980 book, *The Golden Turkey Awards: The Worst Achievements in Hollywood History.* The authors included the star's earnest turn in *The Miracle of the Bells* among the nominees in category of "Worst Performance as a Clergyman or Nun."

Admittedly, it's a bit jarring to see Sinatra wearing priestly vestments in this mawkish religious drama. At the time, however, the star was

> ## "The Archangel Michael, familiarly called Mike throughout the picture, ought to sue."
>
> *Time*

> ## "I know what makes a saint and I also know what makes a beautiful human being."
>
> **Father Paul (Sinatra)**

Left: Father Paul and press agent William Dunnigan (Fred MacMurray).

Right: Sinatra as Father Paul.

in desperate need of an image overhaul. Rumors of his mob ties, coupled with his increasingly hostile relationship with the press, had tarnished Sinatra's reputation. Portraying a man of the cloth may have seemed like a surefire way to generate positive headlines for a change. The RKO-Radio Pictures publicity department went into overdrive, touting the news that Sinatra, the former altar boy, would donate his salary to the Roman Catholic Church. As it turned out, no amount of spin control could disguise the fact that *The Miracle of the Bells* is a leaden amalgam of schmaltzy religious drama and showbiz clichés.

Written for the screen by Ben Hecht, Quentin Reynolds, and Dewitt Bodeen, the film uses a flashback narrative structure to depict the meteoric rise and tragic fall of Pennsylvania mining-town beauty Olga Treskovna (Valli). Plucked from obscurity to star in a film about Joan of Arc, she dies shortly after finishing the film. On the pretext of honoring her dying wish, press agent William Dunnigan (MacMurray) accompanies Olga's body home for burial, but his motives aren't entirely noble. He also plans to drum up maximum publicity for Olga's first and only film by getting the town's churches to ring their bells for three days before the funeral mass, given by Father Paul (Sinatra). The purported "miracle" occurs during Olga's funeral, when statues of the Virgin Mary and Jesus turn to face her coffin. While it's probably a result of seismic activity, induced by coal mining, Father Paul preaches about the miracle of Olga's goodness and devotion to her friends and family.

Sinatra is off screen for long stretches of the film's two-hour running time, but when he appears, he is not at his best in *The Miracle of the Bells*— nor is he at his worst, despite vitriolic reviews to the contrary. He may not be completely persuasive as a coal-mining town priest, but Sinatra doesn't embarrass himself as Father Paul. It was a case of the material failing him and his costars.

Opposite top: Irving Pichel's screen version of Russell Janney's best-selling novel was released in the spring of 1948.

Opposite bottom: Dunnigan comforts the dying Olga (Valli).

THE KISSING BANDIT

AN MGM PICTURE | 1948

Director

Lázló Benedek

Screenplay

John Briard Harding and Isobel Lennart

Principal Cast

Frank Sinatra (Ricardo), Kathryn Grayson (Teresa), J. Carrol Naish (Chico), Mildred Natwick (Isabella), Mikhail Rasumny (Don Jose), Billy Gilbert (General Toro), Sono Osato (Bianca), Clinton Sundberg (Colonel Gomez), Carleton Young (Count Belmonte), Ricardo Montalban, Cyd Charisse, and Ann Miller (Fiesta Specialty Dancers)

EVEN THE MOST ardent Sinatra fans would be hard pressed to find something complimentary to say about *The Kissing Bandit*, which is generally regarded as the worst film of his career. Reviled by critics and ignored by moviegoers when it opened in the fall of 1948, this gaudy embarrassment of an MGM musical comedy paired Sinatra and Kathryn Grayson for the third and final time in a project Sinatra reportedly loathed. In fact, years later the star made his daughter Nancy promise that she would never let his granddaughter, A. J., see *The Kissing Bandit*.

Looking understandably pained for most of the film's running time, Sinatra portrays Ricardo, the milquetoast son of the title character, a legendary outlaw in 1840s-era California. More interested in running a quaint inn than robbing stagecoaches, the Boston-raised Ricardo nevertheless dons his father's signature mask and cape at the prodding of the aging bandito Chico (J. Carrol Naish). During his first robbery, Ricardo botches the job but lands the girl: Teresa (Grayson), the beautiful, sheltered daughter of the Spanish governor (Mikhail Rasumny). Although she can barely contain her excitement at the prospect of a swoon-inducing kiss from the legendary lothario, Ricardo is initially too timid to seal the deal. It's a typically hokey twist in John Briard Harding and Isobel Lennart's simplistic and cliché-ridden screenplay, which traffics in cartoonish racial

"Look at me. If I held you up, would you give me your money?"

Ricardo (Sinatra) to Chico (J. Carrol Naish)

"I think I'm gonna like being a bandit."

Ricardo

"The frenzied members of Frankie's Fan Clubs are not going to be very happy about their Mr. Sinatra's latest picture."

Cue

Left: Ricardo serenades Teresa.

Right: Kathryn Grayson as Teresa, the governor's beautiful daughter.

stereotypes and tired slapstick gags that are equally cringe-inducing. Of course, Ricardo will eventually summon the nerve to plant one on Teresa, but there's no payoff to their romantic clinch—just relief when the screen finally fades to black.

Given the caliber of the talent before and behind the camera—both choreographer Stanley Donen and composer André Previn worked on *The Kissing Bandit*—the ineptitude of the filmmaking is staggering. First-time director Lázló Benedek shows little to no affinity for staging either musical or comedy sequences in this dud that MGM let gather dust on the release shelf for a year before dumping it in theaters. As for Sinatra, he's completely miscast as the quivering and insecure Ricardo who makes his entrance with a pratfall, thrown by a horse through a window. Yet by sheer force of talent, Sinatra manages to rise above the dreck, albeit briefly, when he sings the film's four songs: "If I Steal a Kiss," "Señorita," "Siesta," and the unfortunately titled "What's Wrong with Me?" For a few fleeting moments, the tackiness of *The Kissing Bandit* is forgotten, as Sinatra commands the screen with his velvet-smooth voice.

Opposite bottom: Sinatra and Grayson teamed for the third and final time in *The Kissing Bandit*.

Right: Ricardo and Chico (J. Carrol Naish) plot their next move.

Below: Ricardo tries to follow in his notorious father's footsteps.

TAKE ME OUT
TO THE BALL GAME

AN MGM PICTURE | 1949

Director
Busby Berkeley

Screenplay
Harry Tugend and George Wells

Principal Cast
Frank Sinatra (Dennis Ryan),
Esther Williams (K. C. Higgins),
Gene Kelly (Eddie O'Brien),
Betty Garrett (Shirley Delwyn),
Edward Arnold (Joe Lorgan),
Jules Munshin (Nat Goldberg)

FOR FRANK SINATRA and Gene Kelly, 1949 was big. After pleasing fans in *Anchors Aweigh* four years earlier, the duo teamed up that year for a pair of films: *Take Me Out to the Ball Game* (released in time for opening day) and *On the Town* (a Christmas present for Sinatra and Kelly fans). The latter gets all the attention, but *Take Me Out to the Ball Game* is a fun musical in the grand MGM tradition. It's an energetic dose of wholesome Americana that takes its cue from the vaudeville-style title song performed by the two stars. In fact, a vaudeville spirit pervades the whole film, with Sinatra and Kelly hoofing, singing, and mugging their way through nearly every scene. It's a high-energy romp that succeeds despite a soundtrack that produces no truly memorable songs other than the title tune.

The idea for the film came from Kelly and his friend and collaborator Stanley Donen, who staged the numbers for this baseball-themed musical set around the turn of the century. Busby Berkeley was signed on to direct, and Judy Garland was originally slated to play the female lead. When a drug problem and chronic tardiness led to her dismissal, the next choice was June Allyson, who turned down the part because she was pregnant. Third choice? Esther Williams, who eagerly snapped up the role of rookie baseball team owner K. C. Higgins because it gave the swimming sensation a chance to work outside of the pool and with Sinatra. "I had

> "A breezy affair with a baseball background, this comedy offers a talented cast, some fairly funny lines, musical numbers that are only so-so, and the usual slapstory. Frank Sinatra is developing into quite a comedian, and his scenes with the boisterous Betty Garrett are some of the best in the film."

Mae Tinee, *Chicago Tribune*

Left: Whether they're playing baseball or Boise, O'Brien (Gene Kelly) and Ryan (Sinatra) sing, dance, and joke all the time.

Right: "He thinks he's got muscles." Sinatra's spindly frame inspired a running joke in *Take Me Out to the Ball Game*.

Above: The team's new owner, K. C. Higgins (Esther Williams), shows her players a better way to bat.

Right: Esther Williams went right from being a national AAU swimming champion to Hollywood, where movies such as *Bathing Beauty* showcased her grace under water.

Opposite: Sinatra, Kelly, and Jules Munshin perform "O'Brien to Ryan to Goldberg."

been a bobby-soxer in the early days of Frank's singing career," she wrote in her autobiography. "I bought every record he ever made."

She and Sinatra became "instant friends," which was fortunate because Kelly and Donen resented the fact that they had to resort to a third choice and apparently made Williams the butt of their jokes. Berkeley had his own problems; this would be the last film that the musical wizard would direct and Kelly and Donen handled much of the direction themselves. Sinatra was reportedly afraid that, like Garland, he was going to get canned, because, as Williams put it, "He was a Roman candle shooting off in all directions." After filming finished each day he "went rushing off to one bash or another" and had to take "catnaps" during the day because he'd been out all night. Sometimes he nursed hangovers, but Williams says she told him he had nothing to worry about. "Take a look at the dailies. Your voice sounds wonderful. You're even matching Gene step-for-step in the dance numbers."

He was, too. According to costar Betty Garrett, "Frank worked hard on all the dances; he had a natural grace and moved easily." That's what is most amazing about *Take Me Out to the Ball Game*. Sinatra's in Kelly's world, but he handles himself like a veteran hoofer. These two *could* have played vaudeville as a tandem and made a very successful career out of it.

"And the individual performances of the Messrs. Kelly and Sinatra on this team are genially and frankly in the spirit of unabashed burlesque."

Bosley Crowther, the *New York Times*

Kelly plays Eddie O'Brien, third baseman for the world champion Wolves baseball team, while Sinatra plays second baseman Dennis Ryan. According to a *New York Times* review, their clowning sequences (like one in which they used a gigantic soft bat) were inspired by the antics of real players Nick Altrock and Al Schacht. The film opens with a playbill showing the duo making the rounds as ballplayers capitalizing on their fame by playing the vaudeville circuit together. When spring training begins, they leave the stage and take their shtick back to the diamond, singing "Yes, Indeedy" to their teammates. At a team dinner they include the first baseman from their double play combination for a pleasant-enough "O'Brien to Ryan to Goldberg" song, with Jules Munshin providing even more comedy than Sinatra and Kelly.

The rest of the tunes aren't as catchy. "The Right Girl for Me" is an ordinary little ballad that Sinatra sings to Williams, while "The Hat My Dear Old Father Wore upon St. Patrick's Day" feels like a bowl of sentimental tripe. And "It's Fate Baby, It's Fate" has its lyrics and melody

Opposite: Ryan will go to any length to romance K. C. Higgins.

Above: Überfan Shirley (Betty Garrett) with the object of her affection.

Left: The cast performs the film's big production number, "Strictly U.S.A."

Above: In a rare quiet moment, the boys engage in a little "girl talk," both literally and figuratively.

Left: Sinatra sings "Boys and Girls Like You and Me," a number later cut from the film.

dwarfed by the narrative action. Only the big production number, "Strictly U.S.A.," takes off like the fireworks in a ballpark after a home run.

Thankfully the narrative is much more than an excuse to get to the next song. It features the kind of classic competition over a woman that viewers saw in the Crosby-Hope-Lamour *Road* pictures, with it never being clear until late in the film just who's going to get the main "girl." Since Williams' character is a new owner of the Wolves, she has to prove to the team that she's more than just an heiress, and two-thirds of the double-play combo convince Dennis to try to romance the owner so they can all break curfew. In addition, the narrative is set during the early days of baseball, which means gamblers like Joe Lorgan (Edward Arnold) and attempted World Series' fixes enter into the picture. And finally, shades of *Oklahoma!*, the second female lead is a feisty, loud, aggressive type who adds both comic humor and a rich subplot. Betty Garrett is superb as Shirley Delwyn, a woman who reminds us that the term "fan" derives from "fanatic" as she sets her sights on Sinatra and picks him up . . . literally.

Take Me Out to the Ball Game was a success, with the $2 million film grossing $4 million. Reviews were mildly approving. The *Chicago Tribune* wrote, "The story makes no pretense at authenticity—it's just a vehicle for comedy and music. . . . If you are in the mood for something light, you'll find this movie worth a try." And while *New York Times* reviewer Bosley Crowther praised the big production number and Sinatra's ballad, he added, "For all its high spots, however, the show lacks consistent style and pace, and the stars are forced to clown and grimace much more than becomes their speed." Crowther may have missed the point. Kelly and Sinatra aren't just nervously clowning to fill space. They're carrying on in the tradition of vaudeville that this film celebrates as much as the Great American Pastime. What's more, *Take Me Out to the Ball Game* proved that Sinatra had the chops to be a song-and-dance man, if he had wanted. He had become a legitimate musical comedy star.

Above: "Honest, Eddie, I can explain the whole thing!" Moments later, his friend will chase him around the bases in an unorthodox "hit and run."

Right: The rousing finale of *Take Me Out to the Ball Game*.

ON THE TOWN

AN MGM PICTURE | 1949

Directors
Gene Kelly and Stanley Donen

Screenplay
Adolph Green and Betty Comden

Based on the play by Comden
and Green

Principal Cast
Gene Kelly (Gabey), Frank
Sinatra (Chip), Betty Garrett
(Brunhilde Esterhazy), Ann Miller
(Claire Huddesen), Jules Munshin
(Ozzie), Vera-Ellen (Ivy Smith)

REUNITED WITH his *Take Me Out to the Ballgame* (1949) co-stars, Gene Kelly, Betty Garrett, and Jules Munshin, Frank Sinatra scored a commercial and critical hit with the frothy musical *On the Town* (1949). The film was based on the 1944 Broadway hit musical, which in turn was based on Jerome Robbins's ballet, *Fancy Free*. MGM invested in the Broadway production, which features a score by Leonard Bernstein with book and lyrics by Adolph Green and Betty Comden. However, when MGM studio boss, Louis B. Mayer saw the show, he declared it "smutty" and "communistic." Yet Gene Kelly managed to convince Mayer not only to move forward with the film adaptation with himself and Stanley Donen as co-directors, but to allow the duo the unusual and expensive opportunity to shoot a significant portion of the film on location in New York City.

The decision to shoot in New York results in a vibrancy that is evident right from the start of the film. Opening in the Brooklyn Naval Yard, *On the Town* begins at 6 AM as three sailors come bounding out of their ship and belt out, "New York, New York." (Interestingly, the words of the song are revised from the stage version, "New York, New York, it's a helluva town," to "New York, New York, it's a wonderful town.") Determined to make the most of their twenty-four hour shore leave, Gabey (Gene

"I want to take in the beauties of New York!"

....

Chip (Sinatra)

"And I want to take them out!"

....

Ozzie (Jules Munshin)

"You're awful—awful good to look at, awful nice to be with, awful sweet to have and hold."

....

Chip sings to Brunhilde Esterhazy (Betty Garrett)

Top: Chip, Ozzie (Jules Munshin), and Gabey (Gene Kelly) sing the glories of New York at Rockefeller Center.

Right: Miss Turnstiles (Vera-Ellen), a.k.a. Ivy Smith, meets Gabey in the subway station.

Kelly), Chip (Frank Sinatra), and Ozzie (Jules Munshin), rush to see Manhattan. Chip, a somewhat cerebral fellow, has methodically planned out the day to see the various sites. Gabey and Ozzie are more interested in finding a couple of girls.

While on the subway, the three see a poster for Miss Turnstiles, a.k.a. Ivy Smith (Vera-Ellen), the beauty queen of the month. Gabey becomes enthralled by Ivy's picture and the description of her artistic pursuits. When he tells the others that he's going to meet Ivy, they laugh, but just then, Ivy appears. Gabey introduces himself to her. Ivy is cordial, but quickly runs off to catch a train. Lovestruck, Gabey convinces Chip and Ozzie to help him find her again. The trio winds up in the cab of Brunhilde Esterhazy (Betty Garrett), a confident gal who knows what she wants. She tells the sailors she'll help them, if Chip agrees to sit up front with her.

The group decides to try and find Ivy by going to the cultural places mentioned in the poster. Stopping at an anthropological museum, Ozzie hits it off with a gorgeous, budding scientist, Claire Huddesen (Ann Miller). In an effort to get Chip alone, Brunhilde suggests that they all split up to find Ivy. Ozzie and Claire readily agree. Before separating, they all agree to meet at the Empire State Building at 8:30 PM In the intervening hours, Gabey manages to find Ivy, but when the three couples unite that night to go on the town, events unfold in a way that none of them could have predicted.

Although Sinatra shares top billing with Gene Kelly, there's no question that Sinatra's role is decidedly secondary to Kelly's. Kelly has the central love story and, of course, dazzles with his dancing. Before shooting began, Sinatra's vanity took a hit in a more personal way as well. Not only did he have to wear a hairpiece in the film, but he was forced by MGM brass to wear padding in the rear of his pants because he was deemed too skinny. However, on-screen, there is a salve to his ego. In a throwaway line, Ozzie says to Gabey, "Who you got waiting for you in New York? Ava Gardner?" Sinatra just smiles knowingly at this reference to his real-life affair with the tempestuous movie goddess.

Opposite top: Claire (Ann Miller) compares the measurements of Ozzie with her ideal "Prehistoric Man."

Opposite bottom: The boys get taken for a wild ride by cabbie Brunhilde Esterhazy (Betty Garrett).

> ## "He wanted to see the beautiful sights of our beautiful city of New York. And I showed him plenty."
> **Brunhilde Esterhazy**

On the Town marked the third film in which Frank Sinatra and Gene Kelly shared the screen. In each film, Kelly played a progressively larger role behind the scenes. In *Anchors Aweigh* (1945), Kelly was the choreographer. In *Take Me Out to the Ball Game*, Kelly co-wrote the story and created the choreography with Stanley Donen. In *On The Town,* he and Stanley Donen were the co-directors. Their ambition to shoot a significant portion of the film on location proved historic. Although there had been one or two scenes shot on location in other musicals, no prior musical had the variety of scenes and the artistry that Kelly and Donen brought to the table. The result is that *On the Town* is generally considered the first feature musical shot on location. As Kelly himself remarked, "I really believed it would be a milestone . . . The fact that make-believe sailors got off a real ship in a real dockyard, and danced through a real New York was a turning point in itself." Kelly, Donen, and writers Comden and Green, would go on to even greater cinematic heights with their next film, *Singin' in the Rain* (1952).

For Frank Sinatra, the dancing in *On the Town* was at a more advanced level than he had previously performed, but he gamely rose to the challenge. That said, he was aggravated when Arthur Freed, the head of MGM's musical production unit, cut a poignant song Sinatra's character sings in the stage version. In fact, Freed cut several numbers from the Broadway score and had new songs created by Roger Edens along with Green and Comden. The result of their work was winning the 1949 Academy Award for Best Original Score. *New York Times* critic Bosley Crowther was ambivalent about the music but came to the following conclusion: "From the moment the picture opens . . . the whole thing precipitately moves, with song, dance, comedy, and romance ingeniously interwoven and performed."

Top: Miss Turnstiles agrees to go on a date with Gabey.

Center: Chip tries to fend off Brunhilde's invitation to go to her place.

Bottom: Three's a crowd: Brunhilde's roommate Lucy (Alice Pearce) walks in on Chip and Brunhilde.

Left: The sailors with their dream girls.

Center: Gabey re-imagines his day in New York as a ballet.

Right: Chip and Brunhilde enjoy the top of the Empire State Building.

DOUBLE DYNAMITE

AN RKO-RADIO PICTURE | 1951

Director
Irving Cummings

Screenplay
Melville Shavelson and
Harry Crane

Principal Cast
Frank Sinatra (Johnny Dalton),
Jane Russell (Mildred "Mibs"
Goodhue), Groucho Marx
(Emile J. Keck), Don McGuire
(R. B. "Bob" Pulsifer, Jr.), Howard
Freeman (R. B. Pulsifer, Sr.),
Nestor Paiva ("Hot Horse"
Harris), Frank Orth (Mr. Kofer)

AFTER STARRING in back-to-back MGM musicals, Frank Sinatra opted to make an unpretentious, crowd-pleasing romantic comedy, *Double Dynamite*. A simple story, filmed in black and white and running only eighty minutes, *Double Dynamite* is the kind of film that movie studios made easily at the time, and that audiences just as easily dismissed after a pleasant few hours at a Saturday matinee. But *Double Dynamite* packs more into its short running time than the average post-World War II-era comedy, with uncanny casting and surprising chemistry.

Sinatra portrays earnest bank teller Johnny Dalton, whose fiancée is the comely teller in the next cage, Mildred "Mibs" Goodhue (Jane Russell). Although Johnny's itching to marry "Mibs," he's reluctant to take the marital plunge because of his meager financial situation. His luck takes a turn when he rescues a prominent bookie, "Hot Horse" Harris (Nestor Paiva), from a beating and earns the hoodlum's gratitude and a thousand-dollar reward. While Johnny sits by nervously, Hot Horse begins placing bets for him, and the teller finds himself with $60,000 in cash when the ordeal is over. Before he can break the good news to Mibs, however, it's discovered that a large sum is missing from the bank, so Johnny's windfall, and the anxiety that comes with it, has to be kept under wraps to avoid suspicion. Buoying up the jittery teller is

> "Now look, I work in a bank and I'm not allowed to bet on horses!"

Johnny Dalton (Sinatra) to "Hot Horse" Harris (Nestor Paiva)

Left: Johnny explains to his fiancée Mibs (Jane Russell) why they can't afford to get married.

Right: Johnny can hardly contain himself as he shows off his winnings to Emile (Groucho Marx).

> "The man: Caucasian, brown hair, blue eyes, five-feet-ten, wears elevator shoes, anemic looking, when last seen was wearing ill-fitting suit, well-padded at shoulders, resembles Frank Sinatra."

Police dispatcher calling out an "all points bulletin" for Johnny Dalton (Sinatra)

the wise-cracking waiter Emile J. Keck (Groucho Marx), whose advice to Johnny is to lighten up and take a few risks before life—and his increasingly annoyed fiancée—passes him by. For Mibs, all the talk about big money is the last straw; she's certain it's all a joke, which only adds to Johnny's troubles. As the authorities move in, the heroes lurch from one bailout plan to another, and Johnny becomes so rattled he almost shakes himself right out of his over-sized suit.

For his part in *Double Dynamite*, Groucho Marx delivered a restrained version of the character he had played in more than a dozen Marx Brothers films, toned down to meet the relatively staid Sinatra halfway. In the tradition of great stage comedians, Marx alternates between playing off the other characters and allowing them to get their laughs, a comedic volley that makes everyone look good. In his scenes with Sinatra, Marx quietly slips in his trademark quips as if they're unscripted asides, and keeps his physical comedy in check, only occasionally rolling his eyes and duck-walking across a room. Jane Russell also finds her place in the comic patter of *Double Dynamite*, trading jokes with Marx and keeping the banter snappy in the almost-constant disputes her character has with Johnny. Russell shows off a beautiful singing voice as well when she duets with Sinatra on "Kisses and Tears," and steals a few scenes when Mibs gets drunk on champagne and rambles through a range of emotions from surly to serene.

Despite its charm *Double Dynamite* was not a hit, and the picture's release date was a critical factor. Filmed in 1948, RKO delayed release of the film for three years, and when it finally hit screens on Christmas Day 1951, Sinatra's public image was at an all-time low. Though still married to Nancy Sinatra, the mother of his three children, Sinatra was in the midst of a very public affair with Ava Gardner. The foundations of his career—fans, film studios, and the press—began to turn against him. The teenage bobby-soxers who had made Sinatra a sensation just a few years earlier had grown up and found new idols to embrace. Reporters covered every possible aspect of the stormy Sinatra-Gardner relationship, fueling criticism about celebrities' morals and behavior. Most damaging to

Opposite top: Emile the waiter freely dispenses advice about life and love to Johnny and Mibs.

Opposite bottom: Groucho Marx brought his trademark quips and gags to *Double Dynamite*.

"Johnny, I've been telling you for years, you've gotta learn to enjoy life. Live dangerously. I'll get you the pickled pigs' feet."

Emile J. Keck (Groucho Marx) to Johnny Dalton

Sinatra's reputation, however, was the response by MGM; the studio encouraged Gardner to split with Sinatra, and then dropped him from its roster of stars, buying out the final year of his contract in 1950. Studio head Louis B. Mayer personally delivered the news to Sinatra that he would never work for MGM again.

RKO studio head Howard Hughes was only slightly less punitive. He had allowed Sinatra to be cast in *Double Dynamite* only at the urging of Jane Russell. By delaying release of the film, Hughes had encouraged rumors that Sinatra's career had run its course. Timing for the release of the film appeared almost intentionally harmful to Sinatra, coming a full two years after his previous film, and a month after his well-publicized divorce from Nancy and quick marriage to Ava Gardner. *Double Dynamite* landed in theaters just a month before the release of another Sinatra film, *Meet Danny Wilson*; the lack of strategy behind the dual release was another sign that RKO was not going to invest in Sinatra's future.

Above: Johnny tells Mibs how he came into so much cash.

Opposite top: Before bringing Johnny into his betting parlor, "Hot Horse" Harris (Nestor Paiva) checks in with his Santa Claus lookout for the police.

Opposite bottom: Johnny enlists Emile to help him hide his cash.

Critics recognized that *Double Dynamite* was meant to be a pleasant romp, and graciously reviewed it as such, resisting comparisons to more spectacular Sinatra productions. The film "is prevented from slipping into the category of ordinary film comedy by the sly buffoonery of capable Groucho Marx," wrote Howard McClay in the *Los Angeles Daily News*, adding that "li'l ol' Frank Sinatra, who is held down to two songs, displays quite a knack himself in getting rid of some funny tag lines." *Time* magazine punctured the film's promotion gambit by pointing out that the title was a "leering tribute to the extraordinary physical endowments of actress Jane Russell," though her performance as a modest bank teller ultimately "cheats on RKO's full-bosomed advertising."

Sinatra's grander screen projects would eventually eclipse *Double Dynamite*, but few of his films can match it for its appealing zaniness and undeniable charm. Despite the studio's reservations, it is a film that works on every level, and RKO made a shrewd choice in casting Sinatra with Russell and Marx in the delightful *Double Dynamite*.

"A woman can smell mink through six inches of lead."

Emile J. Keck to Johnny Dalton

Opposite: With the police in hot pursuit, Johnny and Mibs discuss their next move.

Right: Mibs enjoys a bedtime serenade from Johnny—through the wall that separates their apartments.

Below: Johnny is stunned to see Emile stroll into the bank, pretending to be a high roller.

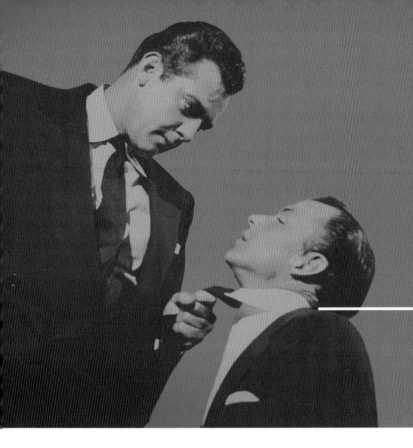

MEET DANNY WILSON

A UNIVERSAL PICTURE | 1951

Director
Joseph Pevney

Screenplay
Don McGuire

Principal Cast
Frank Sinatra (Danny Wilson),
Shelley Winters (Joy Carroll),
Alex Nichol (Mike Ryan),
Raymond Burr (Nick Driscoll)

TO SAY THAT ART imitates Sinatra's life in *Meet Danny Wilson* would be an understatement. The first and only film Sinatra made during his three-year, nonexclusive contract with Universal, this rags-to-riches showbiz saga was written by B-movie actor-turned writer Don McGuire, with considerable input from Sinatra. According to Lawrence J. Quirk and William Schoell's *The Rat Pack: Neon Nights with the King of Cool,* Sinatra took an active role in the screenplay's development, sharing personal stories with McGuire, whom he had befriended during the making of *Double Dynamite.* The entertaining but wildly uneven result is a familiar cautionary tale about a cocky singer's rise and fall that failed to slow the downward trajectory of Sinatra's career in the early 1950s.

Directed by Universal contractee Joseph Pevney, *Meet Danny Wilson* quickly establishes the title character as Sinatra's cinematic alter ego: a physically slight but brash charmer with a temper and prodigious talent to match. Sick and tired of playing cheap dives with his level-headed childhood friend/accompanist Mike Ryan (Alex Nichol), Danny finds an unlikely patron in the menacing form of mobster/nightclub owner Nick Driscoll (Raymond Burr). Introduced to Nick by brassy chanteuse Joy Carroll (Shelley Winters), Danny and Mike land a lucrative gig at Nick's club after Danny wows him by singing "She's Funny That Way."

> ## "You're pretty good. How come you're starving?"

Mobster/nightclub owner Nick Driscoll (Raymond Burr) to Danny Wilson (Sinatra)

> ## "$25 measly bucks for singing your fool head off all night to a bunch of creepy stiffs who don't care if you go blind?!"

Danny Wilson to best friend/pianist Mike Ryan (Alex Nichol)

Left: Joy (Shelley Winters) cleans up Danny after a brawl. There was no love lost between the stars off camera.

Right: Danny holds the room spellbound with his rendition of "She's Funny That Way."

Top: Danny, Nick Driscoll (Raymond Burr), Joy, and Mike (Alex Nichol) celebrate Danny's opening night.

Center: Danny hits the big time.

Bottom: Nick reminds Danny who's boss.

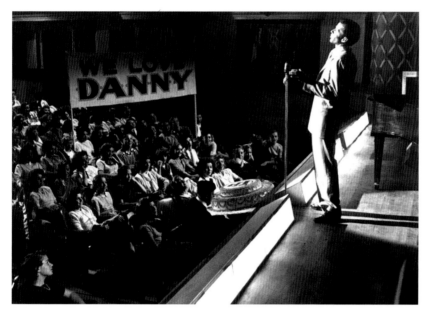

There's just one small hitch: Driscoll wants 50 percent of Danny's future earnings. Despite Mike's misgivings about Driscoll's offer, Danny eagerly agrees to the deal. It's a decision Danny will come to regret once his career takes off, propelling him to the top of the music charts and onto the big screen.

Meanwhile, he's furious when Joy spurns his advances and falls for Mike. Increasingly arrogant and demanding, Danny alienates everyone with his drunken antics and boorish behavior. His career in freefall, Danny decides to sever his ties with Driscoll in a last ditch effort to save his career and reconcile with Mike and Joy.

Although he's never less than mesmerizing when he performs the film's nine songs (his achingly romantic performance of "That Old Black Magic" is especially memorable) Sinatra occasionally overacts in *Meet Danny Wilson*. There's a go-for-broke quality to his performance in certain scenes, as if Sinatra felt this awkward pastiche of thinly veiled musical biopic, noir-esque crime drama, and schmaltzy romance represented his last chance to salvage his film career. That's not to say that he is bad in *Meet Danny Wilson*; in fact, Sinatra and costar Alex Nichol, an original member of the Actors Studio, play off each other with easy assurance and warmth. They're believable as lifelong friends, whereas Sinatra and Shelley Winters have zero chemistry in their scenes together. Nor did they get along off screen. They reportedly clashed frequently and at one point their animosity even became physical. After one particularly heated argument, Winters hauled off and punched Sinatra.

Meet Danny Wilson debuted in the U.K. in 1951, but was not released in the U.S. until the spring of 1952. The movie was received indifferently by critics and filmgoers. Its real-life parallels to Sinatra's tumultuous personal life and career seemingly held faint allure for the public. Unlike the film's title character, who rises from the ashes of his career, newly humbled and grateful, at *Meet Danny Wilson's* conclusion, Sinatra very much remained a fallen star in search of a comeback vehicle in 1952.

"The story cribs so freely from the career and personality of Frank Sinatra that fans may expect Ava Gardner to pop up in the last reel."

Time

Sinatra performs "Old Man River" in
Till the Clouds Roll By.

OTHER SINATRA FILMS
1941–1952

LAS VEGAS NIGHTS
A PARAMOUNT PICTURE · 1941

DIRECTOR	Ralph Murphy
SCREENPLAY	Harry Clork, Ernest Pagano, and Eddie Welch
STORY	Ernest Pagano
PRINCIPAL CAST	Phil Regan (Bill Stevens), Bert Wheeler (Stu Grant), Tommy Dorsey (himself), Constance Moore (Norma Jennings), Virginia Dale (Patsy Lynch)

In this quickie programmer, Sinatra makes an uncredited appearance, singing "I'll Never Smile Again" with the Pied Pipers, Dorsey's female singing group.

SHIP AHOY
AN MGM PICTURE · 1942

DIRECTOR	Edward N. Buzzell
SCREENPLAY	Harry Clork, Irving Brecher, and Harry Kurnitz
PRINCIPAL CAST	Eleanor Powell (Tallulah Winston), Red Skelton (Merton K. Kibble), Bert Lahr (Skip Owens), Virginia O'Brien (Fran Evans), Tommy Dorsey (himself), Frank Sinatra (himself)

Sinatra gets his first screen credit in this unpretentious MGM musical, which features him performing three songs: "The Last Call for Love," "Poor You," and "Moonlight Bay."

REVEILLE WITH BEVERLY

A COLUMBIA PICTURE · 1943

DIRECTOR	Charles Barton
SCREENPLAY	Albert Duffy, Howard J. Green, and Jack Hensley
PRINCIPAL CAST	Ann Miller (Beverly Ross), William Wright (Barry Lang), Franklin Pangborn (Vernon Lewis), Dick Purcell (Andy Adams)

Performing "Night and Day," Sinatra is one of several '40s-era music greats, including Count Basie and Duke Ellington, who appear in this sentimental musical comedy starring tap dancer extraordinaire Ann Miller as an aspiring radio disc jockey.

THE HOUSE I LIVE IN

AN RKO-RADIO PICTURE · 1945

DIRECTOR	Mervyn LeRoy
SCREENPLAY	Albert Maltz
PRINCIPAL CAST	Frank Sinatra (himself)

Sinatra, director Mervyn LeRoy, and producer Frank Ross won an honorary Academy Award for this short film, in which Sinatra teaches a group of schoolyard bullies about the importance of racial and religious tolerance. Sinatra performs two songs in the film, "If You Are But a Dream" and the title track. *The House I Live In*, which was based on Sinatra's idea, was selected for preservation by the National Film Registry in 2007.

TILL THE CLOUDS ROLL BY

AN MGM PICTURE · **1946**

DIRECTORS	Richard Whorf, Vincente Minnelli (uncredited), and George Sidney (uncredited)
SCREENPLAY	Myles Connolly and Jean Holloway
STORY	Guy Bolton
STORY ADAPTATION	George Wells
PRINCIPAL CAST	Robert Walker (Jerome Kern), Van Heflin (James I. Hessler), June Allyson (specialty), Judy Garland (Marilyn Miller), Lena Horne (Julie in *Show Boat*), Kathryn Grayson (Magnolia in *Show Boat*), Van Johnson (Bandleader), Angela Lansbury (Specialty), Tony Martin (Gaylord in *Show Boat*), Virginia O'Brien (Ellie Mae in *Show Boat*), Dinah Shore (Specialty), Frank Sinatra (finale soloist)

In this lavish, highly romanticized biopic about the life and career of composer Jerome Kern, Sinatra concludes the film with his soaring rendition of "Ol' Man River" from *Show Boat*.

Sinatra's career in music and film took off again in the mid-'50s.

PART 2

THE CROONER COMES BACK

1953-1959

BANDLEADER-MUSICIAN Artie Shaw once commented that Frank Sinatra was "a frustrated prize-fighter at heart." Indeed, the son of a professional bantamweight, Sinatra would indulge a fascination with boxing over the years, inviting fighters to join his entourage and occasionally even working out with them. More significantly, though, Sinatra possessed the fundamental traits of

a prize-fighter: the grit, the aggression, the courage, and the swagger. If previous years saw him down and defeated, the 1950s would see him fight back like a champion.

He found the key to his redemption in Fred Zinneman's highly anticipated film version of James Jones's critically acclaimed novel *From Here to Eternity*. Sinatra knew that if he had been born to play any role, it was that of the ill-fated private Angelo Maggio. In 1953, the Motion Picture Academy agreed with Sinatra and awarded him the coveted statuette for Best Supporting Actor. Although some

of the outpouring of industry love might be attributed to Hollywood's fascination with real-life "comeback" stories, Sinatra won the Academy Award over formidable competition, including Jack Palance, who'd earned his second consecutive nomination for *Shane* (1953). All told, *From Here to Eternity* swept the Academy Awards, winning eight statuettes, including Best Picture.

Sinatra followed this triumph with a series of memorable performances, most notably in Otto Preminger's protest against the Motion Picture Production Code, *The Man with the Golden Arm*, which earned Sinatra a second Academy Award nomination. He formed his own production company in 1955 and was named one of the top-ten box office draws in Quigley Publications' annual survey of motion picture exhibitors in 1956—a ranking he would maintain until 1960. But the quiet dedication he had displayed on the set of *From Here to Eternity* seemingly evaporated, and he once again grew impatient with the tedious process of filmmaking.

His true artistry and dedication would find expression in his first love, music. In 1953, he signed with both the William Morris Agency and Capitol Records. A subsequent series of concept albums, many produced in collaboration with Nelson Riddle, would prove to be his finest recordings. Beginning with 1955's *In the Wee Small Hours,* they would explore a deeper, darker side of the singer's persona. Riddle said the best numbers were set to "the tempo of the heartbeat."

But Sinatra could not contain the more brash, aggressive side of his personality that seemed to emerge in times of success. His marriage to Ava Gardner was coming undone. They fought, reconciled, split up again, and spent time in separate places. Newspapers dubbed them the "Battling Sinatras." Both were seen with other people, often for no other reason than to hurt each other. Finally, in 1957, they split for good and filed for divorce.

Sinatra's reputation was not helped by a feud with longtime ally Ed Sullivan, with whom he found himself in bitter dispute over an appearance fee for *The Ed Sullivan Show.* Sinatra lashed out at rock 'n' roll, which he considered the music of "cretinous goons." Despite his success, or perhaps because of it, Sinatra found himself alone, vilified, and confronting the country's rapidly evolving youth culture. Little could he have imagined that one day he'd perform covers of the very songs he hated, including Elvis Presley hits.

During this time Sinatra would form one of his most iconic associations. In 1955, in the wake of a four-day celebration of Noel Coward's opening night in Las Vegas, Lauren Bacall would survey the last of the revelers—Humphrey Bogart, Sinatra, Judy Garland, and David Niven—and proclaim, "You look like a goddamn rat pack."

Bogart's death in 1956 would find Sinatra gravitating to a new group that included Dean Martin, Sammy Davis, Jr., Joey Bishop, and for a time, Peter Lawford. The "relief of boredom" and "perpetuation of independence" around which the original "Clan" had been formed would soon degenerate into frat-boy antics, all covered in scathing detail by the press.

Ava and Frank.

FROM HERE TO ETERNITY

A COLUMBIA PICTURE | 1953

Director
Fred Zinnemann

Screenplay
Daniel Taradash

Based on the novel by
James Jones

Principal Cast
Burt Lancaster (Sgt. Milton Warden), Montgomery Clift (Pvt. Robert E. Lee Prewitt), Frank Sinatra (Pvt. Angelo Maggio), Deborah Kerr (Karen Holmes), Donna Reed (Alma "Lorene" Burke), Philip Ober (Capt. Dana Holmes), Mickey Shaughnessy (Cpl. Leva), Ernest Borgnine (Sgt. "Fatso" Judson)

FRANK SINATRA LOVED the character of Angelo Maggio as soon as he read James Jones's 1951 novel *From Here to Eternity*, but the word in Hollywood was that the film version would never be made. The subject matter was too racy for movie standards of the time, and too violent to earn approval from the military brass, so the project languished until Daniel Taradash turned in a screenplay deemed acceptable by Columbia Pictures. Once director Fred Zinnemann began casting *From Here to Eternity*, however, Sinatra's name was conspicuously absent from the list of actors under consideration to play Maggio; at thirty-eight years old, Sinatra was widely regarded as a has-been. No one could have imagined that this film project would soon earn Sinatra worldwide praise, and a nod from *Variety* for "the greatest comeback in theatre history."

From Here to Eternity is a romantic drama set on and near the Schofield Barracks on Hawaii in the tense months before the attack on Pearl Harbor. At the story's center is Pvt. Robert E. Lee Prewitt (Montgomery Clift), a career military man who has transferred to Hawaii to put his bad luck and bad memories of a boxing accident behind him. When he tells his new leader, Captain Dana Holmes (Philip Ober), that he won't box for the company team, a relentless hazing begins. Holmes's right-hand man, Sgt. Milton Warden (Burt Lancaster), is intrigued by Prewitt's

> ## "It's not confidence, ma'am. It's honesty. I just hate to see a beautiful woman going all to waste."

Sgt. Milton Warden (Burt Lancaster) to Karen Holmes (Deborah Kerr)

Left: Capt. Dana Holmes (Philip Ober) offers Pvt. Robert E. Lee Prewitt a plum position if he agrees to box on the company team.

Right: Frank Sinatra credited Montgomery Clift as a guiding force for his Oscar-winning performance.

> ## "Let's go to a phone booth or something, huh? Where I will unveil a fifth of whiskey I have hidden here under my loose, flowing sports shirt."

Pvt. Angelo Maggio (Sinatra) to Pvt. Robert E. Lee Prewitt (Montgomery Clift)

"Only my friends call me 'wop!'"

Pvt. Angelo Maggio to Sgt. "Fatso" Judson (Ernest Borgnine)

character—the way he loves the military but refuses to conform—and becomes a mentor, watching out for him and offering advice and protection to help him through his ordeal. The two share an emotional weakness as well: They're both involved in off-post relationships, obsessive in nature, and doomed to failure. Warden is carrying on with the captain's wife, Karen Holmes (Deborah Kerr), who freely admits she's slept around, and Prewitt has fallen for Lorene Burke (Donna Reed), a social club hostess whose flirtatious way with soldier-customers increases Prewitt's anxiety by the day. Prewitt's closest friend is Angelo Maggio (Frank Sinatra), a low-level private who is cheerful by nature but short-tempered when insulted or abused; his clashes with the sadistic stockade sergeant, "Fatso" Judson (Ernest Borgnine), fuel the film's heartbreaking subplot. The characters struggle to connect with one another, desperate for affection or control, as we, the audience, anticipate the world-changing events we know are coming soon: A calendar on the wall of Capt. Holmes' office reads "December 6, 1941."

Director Fred Zinnemann, nominated for an Oscar the previous year for his work on *High Noon* (1952), was offered the job of directing *From Here to Eternity* and insisted from the start that he have casting control; without Clift in the lead role, he told studio head Harry Cohn, he refused to be involved. Eventually Zinnemann and Cohn compromised, and

assembled a dream cast that satisfied both. Zinnemann brought on Deborah Kerr, who was known for playing moralistic characters, an image that he knew would make her portrayal of a promiscuous woman infinitely more fascinating to watch. Likewise, he cast wholesome ingénue Donna Reed against type by having her play a nightclub hostess/prostitute. Burt Lancaster was never a point of discussion; both Zinnemann and Cohn considered him their number-one pick. For the part of Maggio, they planned to cast Eli Wallach.

Sinatra hadn't made a film in two years, his record sales had dwindled, and his affair with Ava Gardner and their subsequent marriage had damaged his image tremendously. As his popularity nose-dived, the cheerful confidence that had charmed a nation seemed forever gone. But when he learned that Columbia was casting *From Here to Eternity*, Sinatra proved he still had plenty of fight. He deluged Cohn and Zinnemann with telegrams, insisting that he was perfect for the part and signing his messages "Maggio." Cohn was unimpressed, but a personal appeal from Ava Gardner, a marquee star at the time, convinced him that there was no harm in testing her husband for the part. Sinatra had to pay for his own travel all the way from Africa, where he was staying with Gardner

Opposite top: Tensions between Maggio (Sinatra) and Sgt. "Fatso" Judson (Ernest Borgnine) come to a head.

Opposite bottom: Prewitt falls hard for Lorene Burke (Donna Reed), a hostess at an off-base social club.

Below: Prewitt grinds through fatigue duty, while Warden offers hard-earned advice.

"Man, what I would not give to have this character in a corner poolroom in my hometown."

Pvt. Angelo Maggio talking about
Pvt. Robert E. Lee Prewitt

while she filmed *Mogambo*, but he gladly made the trip. The session went astoundingly well. Sinatra's improvisations were so good that some of his test footage was included in the finished film, but Cohn and Zinnemann were still focused on Wallach, and didn't consider Sinatra seriously until Wallach finally passed on the part.

From Here to Eternity was filmed on Oahu in the spring of 1953. Sinatra came prepared, but found the best possible acting coach in his co-star Montgomery Clift, a Method actor who taught Sinatra how to use posture and gait to convey character, and how to add texture to his performance with small gestures and ticks. In the film, their characters look out for one another and offer encouragement, a dynamic that was helped by the fact that Sinatra and Clift had formed a real friendship off screen, with evenings spent practicing scenes and drinking heavily in their Honolulu hotel.

At the Academy Awards ceremony in March 1954, *From Here to Eternity* carried the evening, winning eight Oscars, including Best Picture, Best Director, Best Screenplay, Best Supporting Actress for Reed, and Best Supporting Actor for Sinatra. From the stage Sinatra told the crowd he was "deeply thrilled and very moved," and alluded to his rough patch of the previous few years by joking, "I'd just like to say, however, that they're doing a lot of songs here tonight, but nobody asked me."

While the evening's winners, and all of Hollywood royalty, headed for the Governors Ball and other opulent celebrations, Sinatra, remarkably, walked away. He headed to the Beverly Hills neighborhood and, all alone, walked up and down the streets. He later explained that he took the time to reflect on his entire life, and everything he had gone through to reach that moment in time. He knew that he would now be recognized as the great actor he'd always hoped to be, and with his new album, *Songs For Young Lovers*, climbing the charts, he knew his singing career was taking an upward turn as well. The second stage of his career had begun, and it would be, Sinatra knew, even better than everything that had come before.

Drunk and happy, Maggio cuts loose with his company comrades. Sinatra campaigned hard to win the role of Maggio in *From Here to Eternity*.

SUDDENLY

A UNITED ARTISTS RELEASE | 1954

Director
Lewis Allen

Screenplay
Richard Sale

Principal Cast
Frank Sinatra (John Baron),
Sterling Hayden (Sheriff Tod
Shaw), James Gleason (Peter
"Pop" Benson), Nancy Gates
(Ellen Benson), Willis Bouchey
(Carney), Kim Charney
("Pidge"), James O'Hara (Jud
Kelly), Paul Frees (Benny),
Christopher Dark (Bart), Paul
Wexler (Deputy Slim Adams)

IN 1954, SINATRA was hitting his stride as a dramatic actor when he took on the difficult role of John Baron, a presidential assassin, in the thriller *Suddenly*, a relatively short (seventy-five minute) noir gem. Bosley Crowther of the *New York Times* called it "a taut little melodrama . . . [that] shapes up as one of the slickest recent items in the minor movie league." and described Sinatra's performance as a "tour de force." *Variety*, typically understated, wrote that having Sinatra portray would-be assassin John Baron was "an offbeat piece of casting which pays off in lively interest."

Indeed it does. Thanks to a taut nail-biter of a script laced with some notably snappy dialogue, Sinatra is eminently believable as an ex-soldier who at one point confesses: "They taught me how [to kill] and I liked it." Sinatra is so convincing, in fact, that many believe the character of John Baron served as an inspiration for Lee Harvey Oswald, who is said to have seen the movie not long before he killed President Kennedy. Hollywood lore has it that Sinatra was so horrified by the alleged link between *Suddenly* and Oswald that he had the film pulled from circulation during the years immediately following JFK's assassination.

Whether the Oswald link is true or apocryphal, the film certainly does eerily foreshadow that fateful day in November 1963. In the film, the sleepy town of Suddenly is set astir by the news that the president is due

"**The laugh is on the guys who are paying the freight. All this loot and they don't even know what they're doing. A half a million clams for absolutely nothing. Because tonight at five I kill the President— one second after five there's a new President. What changes? Nothing. What are they paying for? Absolutely nothing.**"

Would-be assassin John Baron (Sinatra) regales his captives with some of the warped reasoning behind his murderous intentions.

Left: Sinatra as the sadistic would-be assassin Baron.

Right: Posing as FBI agents, Baron and his accomplices worm their way into the Benson home.

at the railroad station that very afternoon at five. He'll be transferring from a train to a car in order to enjoy some recreational time in the nearby mountains. Arriving well ahead of the president is a contingent of Secret Service agents tasked with securing the area to keep the president safe. They mobilize the local sheriff, Tod Shaw (Sterling Hayden), and the state police, and are particularly concerned about a house on the hill above the station from which a gunman might conceivably secure an ideal vantage point to shoot the president.

The house belongs to the Benson family, made up of Ellen Benson (Nancy Gates), a war widow who abhors violence and guns; her young son, "Pidge" (Kim Charney), stifled by his mother's over-protectiveness; and her father-in-law Peter "Pop" Benson (James Gleason), an ex-Secret Service chief who once helped guard President Coolidge before an accident on one of "Cal's" fishing trips forced him to retire.

Into this domestic dynamic come John Baron (Sinatra) and his boys. Posing as FBI agents, they gain access to the Benson home and start sizing up the view from the living room window. "I'm sorry, folks," says Baron, "but I'm afraid we're going to have to hang around for a while." And that they do, though once the sheriff shows up with Secret Service chief Carney (Willis Bouchey), they're forced to abandon their FBI charade and take out their guns, with the tension building exponentially from there.

Of course, if you examine the plot too closely, some things won't add up, but why spoil the ride? There's a great set-up that hinges on Pidge's cap gun, and another that centers on the Bensons' malfunctioning television. And there's some thematic messaging here, too, of the sort you'd expect in a mid-'50s melodrama: the idea that evil is lurking out there, and that no matter where you are, even in a sleepy little hamlet, you'd best be prepared; in fact, it's downright un-American not to be. It's never spelled out exactly who's paying John Baron "half a million clams" to assassinate the commander-in-chief, but given that the film was made in the Cold War Era, it's implicit that the Soviets are behind the plot. For contemporary viewers, *Suddenly* touches upon the hot-button issue of

Top: John Baron and his two accomplices, Benny (Paul Frees) and Bart (Christopher Dark), make their first appearance in *Suddenly*.

Center: Would-be assassin John Baron scopes out the train station where the President of the United States is scheduled to arrive later that afternoon.

Bottom: "Pop" Benson (James Gleason) reveals that he has a silver revolver hidden in the bedroom drawer.

Top: Baron fondly recalls his "choppin" days as a soldier awarded the Silver Star.

Center: Baron forces Ellen (Nancy Gates) to peer through the scope of the rifle.

Bottom: Ellen clutches a kitchen knife and weighs her options under the watchful gaze of her captor.

whether we should all keep guns in our bedrooms. Judging from *Suddenly*, the answer a half-century ago was a resounding "yes," but everything—including "B" movies were, literally and figuratively, a lot more black and white back then.

Filmed partly on location in the Southern California towns of Newhall and Saugus, *Suddenly* opened in the fall of 1954 and made a then-decent $1.4 million at the box office, but it was too small and too short to be more than a blip on Sinatra's lengthy resume. Even so, when he's not spitting out lines that sound pulled from a pulp novel ("Show me a guy with feelings and I'll show you a sucker!"), Sinatra conveys an air of menace that's all the more impressive, given that he's physically rather slight. More often than not, Nancy Gates falls into histrionics worthy of an Eisenhower-era anti-drug film, turning some of her scenes with Sinatra into damsel-villain exchanges reminiscent of the silents. But sparks fly when Sinatra gets to play off of Sterling Hayden as the wounded sheriff with whom he's locked in a game of psychological cat and mouse during the claustrophobic last third of the film.

Suddenly is so claustrophobic, in fact, it could easily have been a play instead of a film. Yet, riding the suspenders of Sinatra's virtuoso performance, the small cast carries it off. Think of *Suddenly* as *Marty* with guns and you won't be disappointed. And think of Ol' Blue Eyes honing his skills in preparation for his great work to come in *The Manchurian Candidate*. Most of all, watch *Suddenly* for what it is, a snapshot of a time when all cars were basically Hummers with fins; when America, reaping the rewards of victory in Europe and Japan, was still facing enemies without and within; and when attention spans were protracted enough that people would sit through two films at a time, creating a market for many a gritty, dark, violent, and smoldering little film like this *Suddenly*.

"Sheriff, the first man they shoot to the moon in a rocket will take pains, too, because that's never been done before. Neither has this."

Psychopathic killer John Baron explains to Sheriff Tod Shaw (Sterling Hayden) why he's got a good shot at being the first man to get away with assassinating a U.S. President.

Baron begins to unravel.

YOUNG AT HEART

A WARNER BROS. PICTURE | 1954

Director
Gordon Douglas

Screenplay
Julius J. Epstein and Lenore Coffee

Principal Cast
Frank Sinatra (Barney Sloan), Doris Day (Laurie Tuttle), Gig Young (Alex Burke), Ethel Barrymore (Aunt Jessie Tuttle), Dorothy Malone (Fran Tuttle), Robert Keith (Gregory Tuttle), Elisabeth Fraser (Amy Tuttle)

FRESH FROM HIS Academy Award-winning comeback in *From Here to Eternity*, Frank Sinatra next opted to make an intimate music film that would showcase the new stage in his singing career. *Young at Heart* pairs him with another great vocalist, Doris Day, but the contrast in their styles only accentuates how far Sinatra was moving from established pop music standards. By letting Sinatra sing without edits or interruptions, Gordon Douglas's remake of *Four Daughters* (1938) becomes more than a love story or a family drama: it's a chance to see a singer, close-up, communicating in a way that had never been seen before.

Young at Heart centers on the Tuttles, a family headed by a perpetually bemused music professor, Gregory (Robert Keith), with help from his sister Jessie (Ethel Barrymore), a hard-edged matriarch who'd rather watch the fights on TV than enjoy the music emanating from her living room. The household is sunny and bright, and so are the dispositions of Gregory's daughters, Fran (Dorothy Malone), Amy (Elisabeth Fraser), and Laurie (Doris Day), who together launch into a sonata for piano, violin, and harp with all the ease of a casual conversation.

A variety of suitors, enchanted by the daughters, the music and the domesticity, linger in the Tuttle household, but they're easily outranked when Gregory invites the arrogant but amusing composer Alex Burke

"You know what a glove man is? I'm a glove man. You shag flies in the hot sun all your life, but you never go to bat."

Barney Sloan (Sinatra) to Laurie Tuttle (Doris Day)

"It's homes like these that are the backbone of the nation. Where's the spinning wheel?"

Barney Sloan to Alex Burke (Gig Young)

Right: In *Young at Heart*, Sinatra introduced a new persona that carried through to his popular recordings.

Left: The master at work—Sinatra sings "Someone to Watch Over Me."

Top: The Tuttle sisters (left to right, Dorothy Malone, Doris Day, and Elisabeth Fraser) make music with their father, Gregory (Robert Keith), conducting.

Center: Laurie (Doris Day) sings a pop song to the chagrin of her father.

Bottom: While digging for clams, Alex Burke (Gig Young) professes his love to Laurie.

Aunt Jessie (Ethel Barrymore) proves she's a match for the surly visitor, Barney Sloan.

(Gig Young) for dinner. He's supposed to be writing a Broadway musical on deadline, but Alex has plenty of free time for Laurie, and before long they're engaged. But when Alex's arranger appears on the scene, commissioned to help him complete his musical, the mood in the household—and in the film—takes a dramatic turn. The arranger is Barney Sloan (Frank Sinatra), a melancholy loner who chains-smokes and slumps around in his rumpled suit and angled fedora, a surly misfit who happens to be a musical genius.

The family is perplexed by Barney because he plays piano and sings so beautifully, yet he's gloomy and anti-social, and seems to prefer it that way. When he's at the keyboard Barney looks through people when they speak to him; the man, as Aunt Jessie puts it, is "something," though the Tuttles are not exactly sure what. Laurie is particularly vexed by Barney, who claims that the Fates are against him no matter what he does, and before she knows it her fascination has turned to love, and her engagement to Alex is off. Barney and Laurie are married, and her insistence that he see the brighter side becomes a full-time job. Whether he's singing in a bar or tinkling on the upright in their tiny apartment, the cloud over his

"Please, Aunt Jessie, don't be hardboiled. It doesn't come off."

Barney Sloan to Aunt Jessie Tuttle (Ethel Barrymore)

head is there to stay. Even with the woman he adores, Barney admits, happiness is just not his thing.

Deceptively cheerful in its opening scenes, *Young at Heart* ventures into dark emotional territory, with Barney's fatalistic outlook coloring every scene in which he appears. It's a perfect setting for a Sinatra singing style that had only emerged in the year prior to the film's release, and that would dominate his recordings for years to come. With lush arrangements by conductor Nelson Riddle, Sinatra's *Songs for Young Lovers* and *In the Wee Small Hours*, both released in 1954, featured vocals that surprised listeners, including those who had followed his career from the start. The sentiments he was exploring in song came with a delivery that was achingly sad and remarkably real; he even allowed his voice to crack at certain tender moments in a song. This important stage in his growth as a vocalist is captured in *Young at Heart*, with Sinatra singing full, uninterrupted versions of such standards as "Someone to Watch Over Me" and "Just One of Those Things." Doris Day also sings beautifully in *Young at Heart*, and joins Sinatra for a superb closing duet, "You, My Love."

Despite the vulnerability he expressed in song, Sinatra was a power player in Hollywood again, and not afraid to use his clout. Early in the production of *Young at Heart*, he clashed with the cinematographer, Charles Lang, whom Sinatra felt was taking too long with lighting set-ups, so Lang was replaced. Sinatra strongly disliked Doris Day's husband, Martin Melcher (a feeling shared by many in the Hollywood community) so he had him banned from the Warner Bros. lot during filming, despite the fact that Melcher and Day were the film's co-producers. Sinatra felt that Melcher was taking advantage of his wife's celebrity and using her to advance his own career; years later, when she learned that Melcher had squandered her fortune, Day may have been inclined to agree. But during the making of *Young at Heart*, Day had little choice but to endure Sinatra's open hostility towards her spouse and still pretend to fall in love with him onscreen. In fact, there was little friction between the stars, as Day and Sinatra admired each other greatly, and had been on friendly terms for years.

Opposite top: Barney stuns Laurie with his insights about her family dynamic.

Opposite bottom: Barney explains to Laurie why he's certain the Fates are against him.

"Sometimes when you're on the outside looking in you see some things other people can't."

Barney Sloan to Laurie Tuttle

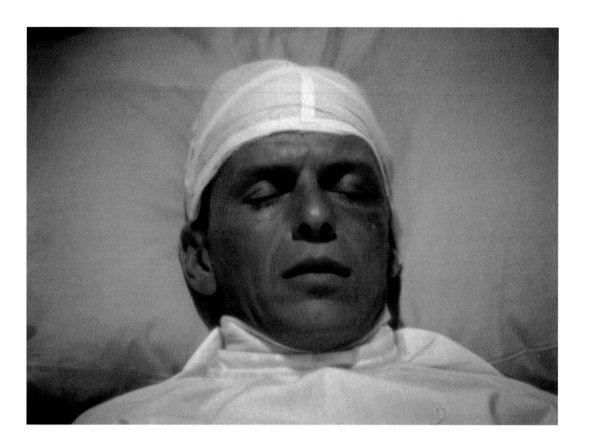

Above: Sinatra as the self-destructive Barney.

Opposite: While the bar crowd ignores him, Barney delivers a heartfelt version of "One for My Baby (and One More for the Road)."

The chemistry between Day and Sinatra, and the enormous fan base each brought to the film, made *Young at Heart* a hit when it opened in December 1954. Some critics sniffed at the fact that the film was a remake of an already good film, but Sinatra received positive reviews for his acting; the reviews of his singing were downright effusive. *Variety*'s review of *Young at Heart* noted that Day and Sinatra "give the songs the vocal touch that makes them solid listening, and score just as strongly on the dramatics, seemingly complementing each other in their scenes together to make the dramatic heart tugs all the more effective."

Soon Sinatra would return to the big Hollywood song-and-dance musicals, and dramas with no singing or dancing at all. But in 1954, when *Billboard* named him top male singer of the year, *Young at Heart* captured a phenomenon before the innovator would move on to something new.

NOT AS A STRANGER

A UNITED ARTISTS RELEASE | 1955

Director

Stanley Kramer

Screenplay

Edward Anhalt and Edna Anhalt

Based on the novel by Morton Thompson

Principal Cast

Robert Mitchum (Lucas Marsh), Olivia de Havilland (Kristina Hedvigson), Frank Sinatra (Alfred Boone), Gloria Grahame (Harriet Lang), Broderick Crawford (Dr. Aarons), Charles Bickford (Dr. Dave W. Runkleman)

AT 948 PAGES, Morton Thompson's 1954 novel *Not as a Stranger* was literally massive. It was also a number-one bestseller, so the press followed every move on the film's road to production. The *Los Angeles Times* reported that producer/director Stanley Kramer wanted sensitive Montgomery Clift for the lead, creating a controversy when laconic Robert Mitchum eventually won the role. The movie also offered Frank Sinatra another opportunity to shine. Fresh off his Best Supporting Actor Oscar win for *From Here to Eternity* (1953), he would take another supporting role as Mitchum's best friend.

Lucas Marsh (Mitchum) is a brilliant medical student who believes that doctors should serve their communities, not line their pockets. Nevertheless he marries nurse Kristina Hedvigson (Olivia de Havilland) for her money when he cannot pay his tuition. His coldness appalls his pal, fellow student Alfred Boone (Sinatra), while his arrogance dismays his teachers. As he starts his career, Lucas is impervious to the criticism. His attitude easily brings on trouble, both in his marriage and medical practice.

High Noon producer Kramer sought a high level of verisimilitude for his directorial debut, insisting that his stars spend time observing real surgeons at work. As sobering as that education might have been, the serious Kramer found himself surrounded by a gang of cut-ups and drunks.

"You can't learn about blood tests from an outline, Alfred. If you don't watch it, they're going to drop you."

Lucas Marsh (Robert Mitchum) chastising friend Alfred Boone (Sinatra) for his poor study habits

"You know the thing that kills me about you, Marsh, is just how far you'll go. I'm supposed to be the cynical type, but I could never do a thing like this. You're letting yourself be kept."

Alfred expressing his shock that Lucas has married for money

Left: Alfred Boone is appalled by the change in Lucas Marsh.

Right: Medical school classmates Alfred Boone and Lucas Marsh take radically different approaches to their studies.

Opposite top: Sinatra with fellow screen greats Robert Mitchum and Olivia de Havilland in Stanley Kramer's adaptation of Morton Thompson's novel.

Opposite bottom: Drunken antics and practical jokes reigned on the set of *Not as a Stranger*. Co-star Lee Marvin (at Sinatra's left) kept pace with Sinatra and Mitchum.

> **"The exceptional cast helps to while away the platitudes and pieties, provided you can accept the likes of Mitchum, Sinatra, and [Lee] Marvin as somewhat wrinkly students."**
>
> Tom Milne, *Time Out Film Guide*

"It wasn't a cast, so much as a brewery," admitted Mitchum. Practical jokes and jibes were a fact of life on set. Sinatra particularly enjoyed ragging much larger costar Broderick Crawford. One day he took the needling too far and filming had to be suspended so that Sinatra could be fitted for a new toupée; in a fit of rage, Crawford ripped the wig from his costar's head and ate it!

The shenanigans upset Kramer, who vowed to never work with Sinatra again, a promise that lasted only until he directed Sinatra in *The Pride and the Passion* two years later. In spite of the trouble, he praised the volatile star's acting chops. "Sinatra's range is fantastic," he said. "He can do anything. He is no longer a singer, but an actor who does songs. As a world star, he could beat Brando."

Sinatra came away from the film with a BAFTA (the British equivalent of the Academy Award) nomination for Best Foreign Actor, but he was one of the few actors to emerge triumphantly from the wreckage. The critics met *Not as a Stranger* with derision. Bosley Crowther dismissed it as "labored," while *Time* complained that "the sudsy vapors of soap opera cloud the film." Mitchum's reviews were even more disastrous. Crowther called him "flat." *Variety* declared, '[Mitchum's] clearly over his acting depth." Sinatra's notices were considerably brighter. *Time* praised the actor's wit and *Variety* suggested that he "comes close to doing a little picture stealing."

Despite the poor reviews, *Not as a Stranger* was a hit, earning more than $6 million at the box office in domestic returns. Mitchum credited Sinatra with its success. His costar, he said, "saved the film."

GUYS AND DOLLS

AN MGM PICTURE | 1955

Director
Joseph L. Mankiewicz

Screenplay
Joseph L. Mankiewicz

Based on the play by Jo Swerling
and Abe Burrows, music and
lyrics by Frank Loesser

Principal Cast
Marlon Brando (Sky Masterson),
Jean Simmons (Sarah Brown),
Frank Sinatra (Nathan Detroit),
Vivian Blaine (Miss Adelaide),
Robert Keith (Lt. Brannigan),
Stubby Kaye (Nicely-Nicely
Johnson), B. S. Pully (Big Jule),
Johnny Silver (Benny
Southstreet), Sheldon Leonard
(Harry the Horse)

FRANK SINATRA takes third billing in the film version of *Guys and Dolls* and ends up stealing the show. In a film that is deliberately two-dimensional, with cartoon-like sets and costumes in every color of the rainbow, Sinatra creates a multidimensional character who naturally becomes the focus of attention every time he appears onscreen. As the crap game operator Nathan Detroit, he has a lot on his mind, and it shows in every twitch and grimace: He's a criminal with a code of honor, a fiancé with a million excuses, a long-shot gambler, a street-life philosopher, and a nervous wreck, all rolled into one.

Based on the stage musical and featuring songs by Frank Loesser, *Guys and Dolls* is a fantasy set in New York's Times Square, and populated with an underworld menagerie of gamblers, thieves, and con artists. Nathan Detroit is a celebrity among the riffraff, known as the operator of the "oldest established permanent floating crap game in New York," and a man badly in need of a few fresh angles. He must have a thousand dollars to get the game started, and a location that will elude Lt. Brannigan (Robert Keith), the officer determined to shut him down. At the same time, his fourteen-year engagement to nightclub singer Miss Adelaide (Vivian Blaine) is wearing thin, and she's liable to leave him if he doesn't quit the underworld life and tie the knot.

> "It does not seem possible—me without a livelihood. Why, I have been running the crap game since I was a juvenile delinquent."

Nathan Detroit (Sinatra) to Nicely-Nicely Johnson (Stubby Kaye) and Benny Southstreet (Johnny Silver)

> "Nathan, no matter how terrible a fellow seems, you can never be sure that some girl won't go for him. Take us."

Miss Adelaide (Vivian Blaine) to Nathan Detroit

Left: With high rollers in town, Nathan Detroit is desperate to find a location for the big game.

Right: Miss Adelaide launches into a sneezing fit as her fiancé, Nathan Detroit, delivers his usual litany of excuses.

Into the picture comes high-roller Sky Masterson (Marlon Brando), who explains to Detroit that he can get any woman he wants, a boast that quickly turns into a $1,000-bet: To save face, and the money, Masterson is challenged to take Save-a-Soul Mission worker Sarah Brown (Jean Simmons) with him to Havana. While Detroit waits for his bet to pay off, his regulars pressure him for the secret location of the big game, which turns out to be in the back of the mission one night and in a sewer the next. Along the way, Detroit and his sidekicks Nicely-Nicely Johnson (Stubby Kaye) and Benny Southstreet (Johnny Silver) sing about the delights of gambling and the pitfalls of marriage; Masterson and Brown sing about the mysteries of love; and Miss Adelaide sings about the life she is throwing away waiting for Detroit to get down on one knee to propose instead of on both knees to roll the dice.

Guys and Dolls had been an enormous hit on Broadway, winning the Tony Award for Best Musical and running for 1,200 performances. Hollywood, however, had a different approach to musicals, and the show underwent major changes on the way to the screen. Several of Loesser's songs from the original were dropped, and he was recruited to add new ones, including "Adelaide," a love song for Sinatra to sing. On stage the Miss Adelaide character was frumpy and whiny, but for the film the part was sexed up with revealing outfits and a salacious production number around a new song, "Pet Me Poppa."

But important elements of the stage musical were carried over, namely a group of fine musical actors who originated their roles, including Vivian Blaine, Stubby Kaye, and Johnny Silver. B. S. Pully also reprised his role as a big-time hoodlum, brilliantly creating an oft-imitated template for comic wise guys on film. On Broadway, the part of Sky Masterson earned a Tony Award for Robert Alda. After only four years in films, Marlon Brando was already a three-time Oscar nominee for Best Actor and one-time winner for his performance in *On the Waterfront*. A box-office name to boot, Brando was signed to replace Alda, despite his limited singing ability. Sinatra, in the smaller role of Nathan Detroit, was a more obvious casting choice: an Oscar-winning actor who also happened to be one of the most celebrated singers in the world.

Top: Nathan Detroit and a chorus of gamblers sing the praises of their beloved "floating" crap game.

Center: Sky Masterson works his charms on mission worker Sarah Brown (Jean Simmons).

Bottom: Sky Masterson advises Nathan Detroit to take a stand against the marriage trend.

Top: Sinatra sings the title song along with original Broadway cast members Stubby Kaye (as Nicely-Nicely Johnson, center) and Johnny Silver (as Benny Southstreet).

Center: Sky Masterson introduces the innocent Sarah Brown to the delights of a rum-spiked Cuban "milkshake."

Bottom: Vivian Blaine, who originated the role of Miss Adelaide on Broadway, delivers the musical ultimatum, "Take Back Your Mink."

The role of Nathan Detroit seems tailor-made for Sinatra's talents, but he had actually hoped for the Sky Masterson role. He had also lost out to Brando for the lead in *On the Waterfront*, and had developed a resentment that continued throughout the production of *Guys and Dolls*. To director Joseph L. Mankiewicz, Sinatra referred to Brando as "Mumbles," and asked to be called to the set only after Brando had completed his lengthy rehearsals, a technique that Sinatra found tiresome and anathema to his more spontaneous approach. Animosity between the stars continued for decades; Brando later referred to Sinatra as a complainer and a hot head, and Sinatra continued to joke, more than forty years after *Guys and Dolls* came out, that Brando couldn't sing. But the professionalism of both actors carried them through the film's production, and any rift on the set is invisible onscreen. Their scenes together have a natural flow and comic timing that make both actors shine, especially in their extended scene at Mindy's restaurant, the gangster hangout, when Masterson explains his philosophy about "dolls," and Detroit, desperate for cash, tries to place a bet about the relative popularity of cheesecake versus strudel.

Big Jule (B. S. Pully) and his "no spots" dice become the undoing of Nathan Detroit.

Released in November 1955, *Guys and Dolls* was an enormous hit and another critical success for Sinatra, whom reviewers singled out for the exceptional blend of talents he brought to the role. Jack Moffitt wrote in the *Hollywood Reporter* that "the way he can tailor a Frank Loesser song is nobody's business but his own," and Hollis Alpert in the *Saturday Review* stated simply that "Sinatra is Sinatra and in this is perfect." *Los Angeles Examiner* columnist Louella Parsons wrote that "the Detroit role is a breeze for Sinatra, and he plays it as casually as if he were eating a banana split."

Brando got the close-ups and the long, romantic scenes, but Sinatra is the real show in *Guys and Dolls*. While his top-billed costars coo and cuddle under a Havana moon, Sinatra keeps things moving as he bounds through crowded streets, restaurants, and barber shops, orbited by an assortment of characters anxious to see what he's going to do next. Then and now, Sinatra has the same effect on anyone watching *Guys and Dolls*.

THE TENDER TRAP

AN MGM PICTURE | 1955

THE TENDER TRAP is like a time capsule. Inside it are swingers, martinis (lots of them), bachelor pads, and the outdated notion that all women, even "career girls," want a husband and three children more than anything else.

Released just three days after *Guys and Dolls* debuted, this film is a milestone for Frank Sinatra because it is the first comedy in which he played the lead role. Though he was married to Ava Gardner at the time, *The Tender Trap* was a movie that made fans think they were seeing the "real" Sinatra—the glamour boy the paparazzi covered, the "ring-a-ding-ding" guy who lived a life that most men could only dream about. And that's the point of this film. It's a battle-of-the-sexes romantic comedy that glorifies the swinging bachelor's life while selling marriage as its prime commodity.

Sinatra plays Charlie Reader, a New York theatrical agent who gets an unexpected visit from his best friend, Joe McCall (David Wayne). Joe is married but recently estranged, and with no place to go he turns up at the high-rise apartment of his friend. Not only does he stay, but Charlie makes him earn his keep by being his secretary at home—no easy feat, considering that Charlie is dating seemingly all the single women in New York. A wide-eyed, open-mouthed Joe watches a revolving door of beautiful women come into and out of Charlie's bachelor life. His dates aren't

Director
Charles Waters

Screenplay
Julius J. Epstein

Based on the play by Max Shulman

Principal Cast
Frank Sinatra (Charlie Y. Reader),
Debbie Reynolds (Julie Gillis),
David Wayne (Joe McCall),
Celeste Holm (Sylvia Crewes),
Jarma Lewis (Jessica Collins),
Lola Albright (Poppy Masters),
Carolyn Jones (Helen)

> **"Colorful as a bright new lipstick and as merry as a sixth martini."**
>
> *Hollywood Reporter*

Ladies' man Charlie Reader (Sinatra) with his latest squeeze Poppy (Lola Albright) and best friend Joe McCall (David Wayne).

> **"You see a pair of laughing eyes And suddenly you're sighing sighs. You're thinking nothing's wrong. You string along, boy, then snap! Those eyes, those sighs, they're part of the tender trap."**
>
> From "(Love Is) The Tender Trap" (Sammy Cahn and Jimmy Van Heusen)

garden variety. No sir. Among the most recent are an editor at Doubleday and a buyer for a big department-store chain. They're all successful career women with one thing in common: They came to New York wanting a career, but still ended up craving marriage. And Charlie has been making a career out of taking advantage of them all, even Jessica (Jarma Lewis), who brings him rare cheeses; Poppy (Lola Albright), who comes bearing whitefish; and Helen (Carolyn Jones), who walks his dog for him. But the wisest among them is Sylvia (Celeste Holm), the only female violinist in the NBC Orchestra. She knows the score, whether there are musical notes or not, and she's the one who also captures the fancy of Charlie's suddenly single (minded) friend.

The basic premise of the film, Sinatra's first for MGM in five years, is crudely but succinctly voiced by Joe: "For all the girls you fondled and forgot, you're being paid back." It is business as usual for Charlie until he runs into a twenty-two year old with a "marriage plan." The woman who finally exasperates him is a young actress named Julie Gillis (Debbie Reynolds), whose plan dictates that she not waste time having dinner with anyone who doesn't strike her as a possible spouse, and who's determined to marry by a predetermined date. So why would a guy like Charlie be interested in a small-town stiff with old-fashioned ideals, other than the fact that she's great-looking? Maybe because she won't play his game, or because she gives him the biggest backhanded compliment he's ever heard: "You're even attractive in an offbeat, beat-up sort of way." So as Charlie pursues Julie, Joe gets into an ever-more confusing situation with Sylvia. Eventually, the romantic merry-go-round leads to major confusion for Charlie, and to a double proposal. "You know more about how to please a lady than any man on the eastern seaboard," Joe says, but that's not the way Julie sees it. She says, "I'm gonna try to make a man out of you, because that's what I want to marry: a man."

In this battle of the sexes, Joe has a ringside seat, and his reaction shots form a running commentary. His bemusement becomes ours, while his asides are drier than the martinis he drinks. The sharpest writing and exchanges occur between Charlie and Joe and when Sylvia joins them.

Top: Sinatra and Academy-Award winner Celeste Holm as Sylvia, the only female violinist in the NBC Orchestra.

Center: "Watch this kid, Charlie. The office signed her last week."

Bottom: So why isn't Julie Gillis (Debbie Reynolds) more excited about landing her first big part? Because theater is just a temporary thing . . . until *marriage*.

Top: After Julie performs "The Tender Trap" in rehearsal, Charlie shows her how it's supposed to be done.

Center: Charlie the perennial bachelor takes a seat in a modern living room designed for a family of five.

Bottom: Everything comes full circle as the title song is sung one last time.

When these three characters are onscreen together the film is at its smartest. *The Tender Trap*, adapted from a Broadway play by Max Shulman, sags in the second act before the resolution, but otherwise it's an engaging outing for Sinatra and the rest. It's sexist, sure, but then again very few films weren't in the 1950s.

When Reynolds is on-camera, the film gets preachy. Despite her willingness to "neck," her character is the standard bearer for small-town values. But there are lines related to the married vs. single life debate scattered throughout: "There are worse things for a girl than not getting married," Joe says to Sylvia, who snaps, "Name three." And we get this little gem from Sylvia, "The only way to have a girl is not to marry her." Julie is offended that all of Charlie's girlfriends picked him up at his apartment or met him at a public place, and she expects him to come to her house to call for her. For a forward "girl" she's awfully naïve, and this too adds to the film's quaint time-capsule feeling.

Sinatra sings the film's title song.

"The Tender Trap" received an Academy Award nomination for Best Original Song, but lost out to "Love is a Many-Splendored Thing." It's a catchy tune, especially the way Sinatra sings it, but it almost wears out its welcome. We hear it from Sinatra in the pre-title sequence, by the four principal stars in a postscript finale, and by Reynolds and Sinatra mid-film during rehearsal scenes for the show in which Reynolds's character stars. We also get symphonic strains of the title track that move the action along throughout the film. The saturation level is so intense that by the end, you're either going to love the tune or hate it, but either way, you won't be able to get it out of your head. Capitol Records released the song as a single with "Weep They Will" on the B-side, and as a song on an album, *This is Sinatra!*, the following year.

At one point Julie remarks that this is "the atomic age," and though *The Tender Trap* isn't one of Sinatra's best films, it's no bomb either. Two years after Sinatra proved he was a serious dramatic actor in *From Here to Eternity,* he proved in *The Tender Trap* that he was also a bankable lead actor for a comedy.

THE MAN WITH THE GOLDEN ARM

A UNITED ARTISTS RELEASE | 1955

Director
Otto Preminger

Screenplay
Lewis Meltzer and Walter
Bernstein

Based on the novel by
Nelson Algren

Principal Cast
Frank Sinatra (Frankie Machine),
Eleanor Parker (Zosch Machine),
Kim Novak (Molly), Arnold
Stang (Sparrow), Darren
McGavin (Louis)

IN 1955, SINATRA TACKLED what is undeniably the most demanding role of his entire film career: Frankie Machine, the aspiring jazz drummer struggling to quit heroin in *The Man with the Golden Arm*. Never again would Sinatra immerse himself so completely in a role as he did in Otto Preminger's adaptation of Nelson Algren's novel, winner of the first National Book Award in 1949. In fact, Sinatra had been so anxious to do Preminger's film, and to beat out his despised rival Marlon Brando for the title role, that he'd committed to the project after reading only the first fifty pages of Walter Newman's script.

For Sinatra, playing Algren's vulnerable anti-hero would be sweet revenge on Brando, who had snared not one, but two lead roles Sinatra coveted: Sky Masterson in *Guys and Dolls* (1955) and Terry Malloy in *On the Waterfront* (1954). Producer Sam Spiegel had originally cast Sinatra as Malloy, a washed-up ex-boxer turned Hoboken dockworker, but had reneged on their "handshake deal" to sign Brando, then a bigger box-office draw than Sinatra. Furious, Sinatra had retaliated by suing Spiegel for breach of contract; the case was later settled amicably out of court.

Yet for all his enthusiasm about *The Man with the Golden Arm*, Sinatra was nevertheless somewhat apprehensive about working with Preminger, a filmmaker respected and reviled in equal measure. Although he'd won great

> **"The monkey is never dead, Dealer. The monkey never dies. When you kick him off, he just hides in a corner, waiting his turn."**
>
> Louie (Darren McGavin) to Frankie Machine (Sinatra)

> **"I'm the kind of guy, boy when I move, watch my smoke. But I'm gonna need some good clothes though."**
>
> Frankie Machine

> **"A gripping, fascinating film."**
>
> *Variety*

Left: Sinatra received his second Academy Award nomination for playing Frankie, the vulnerable drug addict who dreams of becoming a jazz drummer.

Right: Kim Novak gives a touching performance as Molly, the sad-eyed nightclub hostess.

Clean and sober, Frankie (Sinatra) tries to avoid Louie (Darren McGavin), his former drug dealer.

acclaim for such films as *Laura* (1944) and *Carmen Jones* (1954), Preminger was a volatile control freak, seemingly cut from the same dictatorial mold as fellow Austrian filmmaker Erich Von Stroheim. Indeed, Preminger's on-set tirades had earned him the nickname "Otto the Terrible." That Billy Wilder had cast Preminger as the commander of a Nazi prison camp in *Stalag 17* (1953) struck many in Hollywood as art imitating life.

Conversely, Preminger had reservations about Sinatra, whose rumored mob ties and hair-trigger temper were already the stuff of tabloid legend. As Preminger later told writer Evelyn Harbert in a 1956 *Parade* magazine profile, "The Man Who Changed the Moral Code [Sinatra], has a chip on his shoulder all the time. And unlike most stars, he doesn't really get along with little people."

Given their notorious reputations, it seemed a foregone conclusion that Sinatra and Preminger would clash loudly and repeatedly while filming *The Man with the Golden Arm*. To the surprise of everyone in the film community, however, director and star worked together beautifully, with a minimum of friction. The anticipated screaming matches never erupted between Sinatra and Preminger, who genuinely liked each other, so much so that they gave each other nicknames: Sinatra dubbed Preminger "Ludwig," while Preminger christened his star "Anatol," after the womanizing title character of Arthur Schnitzler's 1893 play.

Top: Eleanor Parker as Zosch, Frankie's grasping, manipulative wife.

Center: Frankie finds himself drawn to Molly, who's the antithesis of Zosch. Normally resistant to doing multiple takes, Sinatra was atypically patient with Novak, who repeatedly flubbed her lines.

Bottom: Frankie botches his audition at a jazz club.

Top: The harrowing "cold turkey" sequence. To prepare, Sinatra watched a drug addict drying out in a padded cell.

Center: Zosch makes a final, desperate attempt to hold onto Frankie.

Bottom: Frankie reluctantly deals cards in an illegal poker game.

That said, the apparent lovefest between director and star didn't extend to the rest of the cast and crew filming *The Man with the Golden Arm* on the RKO back lot (location shooting in Chicago had been nixed, due to budgetary concerns). At one point in the tight, thirty-day production, Preminger delivered such a blistering critique of cast member Darren McGavin's performance as Louie, the predatory neighborhood drug dealer, that the actor reportedly "chased him [Preminger] up the boom." Sinatra also blew up at a set electrician, whom he tried to get fired, but Preminger refused to cater to his star's demands.

Whereas Preminger ran roughshod over McGavin and character actor Arnold Stang, he was uncharacteristically patient and nurturing with newcomer Kim Novak, then being groomed for stardom by Columbia Pictures studio head Harry Cohn. Cast as Molly, the compassionate nightclub hostess who acts as Machine's refuge from his manipulative, wheelchair-bound shrew of a wife Zosch (Eleanor Parker, on loan from MGM), Novak was so nervous and insecure that she often required upwards of thirty takes to get through a scene without flubbing her lines. Fortunately, Novak's lack of technique was more than offset by her innate charisma; Preminger recognized a sad-eyed, dreamy quality in Novak that perfectly complemented Sinatra's down-to-earth yet vulnerable performance.

Although he famously hated doing multiple takes, Sinatra held his notorious temper in check with Novak, no matter how many times she froze while shooting their scenes together. Then again, he flatly refused to do a second take on one of the film's pivotal scenes: desperate for a fix, Machine attacks Louie, knocking him out with a chair, and then ransacks the dealer's tenement apartment looking for drugs. Nor would Sinatra do more than one take of Machine's last-ditch attempt to go "cold turkey," locked up in Molly's apartment, because he knew he nailed this physically and emotionally draining scene the first time, *without* benefit of rehearsal.

Not that Sinatra was winging it. To convey the agony of Machine's withdrawal from heroin with maximum authenticity, Sinatra had observed

Frankie looks to Molly for emotional support.

Top: *The Man with the Golden Arm* shocked 1950s audiences with its graphic portrayal of drug addiction.

Center: In jail on a trumped-up charge, Frankie begins to crack.

Bottom: Sinatra studied jazz drumming to play Frankie in Otto Preminger's adaptation of Nelson Algren's novel.

an addict drying out in a padded cell. As he later told writer Val Robins in a 1989 interview, the experience had left him deeply shaken: "The poor kid was out of his head. I couldn't handle it, I walked away, I couldn't control myself. To see the actual thing was scary, but it helped me when we started shooting. I knew what I wanted to do."

Sinatra's intense preparation for the role—he'd even learned to play drums from jazz great Shelley Manne—earned him critical raves when *The Man with the Golden Arm* premiered on December 14, 1955, sans approval from the Production Code, which then strictly prohibited the depiction of drug addiction and trafficking onscreen. The film itself received mixed notices. Although *Variety* hailed *The Man with the Golden Arm* as "a gripping, fascinating film," The *New York Times*' Bosley Crowther dismissed Preminger's taboo-busting adaptation of Algren's novel as "a pretty plain and unimaginative look-see at a lower-depths character with a perilous weakness for narcotics." Algren himself loathed the film, which Preminger transformed from a relentlessly downbeat character study into a redemption saga that ends on a positive note. Audiences, however, flocked to *The Man with the Golden Arm,* turning it into one of the most profitable films of 1956.

Today, when films such as *Requiem for a Dream* (2000) portray the horrors of drug addiction in graphic, unflinching detail, *The Man with the Golden Arm* looks downright quaint by comparison. But while the years have not been kind to Preminger's film, which is now chiefly remembered for its successful challenging of the Production Code rather than its cinematic artistry, Sinatra's Oscar-nominated performance has lost none of its raw power.

JOHNNY CONCHO

A UNITED ARTISTS RELEASE | 1956

Director

Don McGuire

Screenplay

Don McGuire and David P. Harmon

Based on the teleplay "The Man Who Owned the Town" by Harmon

Principal Cast

Frank Sinatra (Johnny Concho), Keenan Wynn (Barney Clark), William Conrad (Tallman), Phyllis Kirk (Mary Dark), Wallace Ford (Albert Dark), Dorothy Adams (Sarah Dark), Christopher Dark (Walker)

FOUR YEARS AFTER they worked together on *Meet Danny Wilson*, Sinatra and writer Don McGuire reteamed to make *Johnny Concho*, an off-beat western that's a genuine curio among Sinatra's films. Never one to shy away from taking risks onscreen, Sinatra portrays the title character, a craven bully in Arizona, circa 1875, who gradually develops both a back-bone and conscience when two outlaws threaten his community. And while he's not altogether persuasive as a nineteenth-century wannabe gun-slinger, Sinatra nevertheless deserves credit for at least attempting to stretch as an actor in *Johnny Concho*.

Produced by Sinatra, McGuire's directorial debut is a stilted, inter-mittently involving adaptation of a 1954 episode of the CBS anthology series, *Studio One*. The narrative unfolds against the backdrop of the fron-tier town Cripple Creek, Arizona, where the skinny runt Johnny Concho would be a pariah—if the locals didn't fear the wrath of Concho's outlaw brother Red. Taking full advantage of his brother's infamy, Johnny does whatever he wants without fear of retribution. That is, until the outlaws Tallman (William Conrad) and Walker (Christopher Dark) ride into Cripple Creek and announce they've killed Red. When Tallman challenges him to a duel, Johnny flees town. Only through the love and support of local girl Mary Dark (Phyllis Kirk, who replaced

> "*Johnny Concho* was my first attempt at producing a picture. And all of us worked very hard to give you what we earnestly hope is an exciting, colorful western movie."

Sinatra in the film's trailer

> "Congratulations. You just bought yourself a $300 rat."

Johnny (Sinatra) to Mary Dark (Phyllis Kirk)

Left: Mary Dark (Phyllis Kirk) is the only one who believes in Johnny.

Right: Sinatra as the title character of this offbeat western, written and directed by his friend Don McGuire.

Gloria Vanderbilt), does Johnny find the strength to change from mouthy bully to unlikely hero, willing to defend Cripple Creek against Tallman and his sidekick.

Far too talky for its own good and slightly claustrophobic in a stage-like setting, *Johnny Concho* failed to connect with either Sinatra fans or devotees of the western genre. Sinatra certainly tried to generate maximum publicity for the film's world premiere at the Paramount Theatre in New York. He reunited with bandleaders Jimmy and Tommy Dorsey to perform for a week at the Paramount, but to little commercial avail. Apparently, the prospect of seeing Sinatra play a lying, cheating punk held faint allure for audiences in 1956.

Granted, it takes a colossal suspension of disbelief to accept the Hoboken native as a nineteenth-century frontier character, but Sinatra does pretty well in the title role. Reviewers were admiring, if not enthusiastic about his performance. Philip K. Scheur of the *Los Angeles Times* wrote, "Performing competently if not brilliantly, he at least causes one to dislike him at the start and pull for him at the finish."

Viewed today, Sinatra's first and only serious western qualifies as an interesting failure. The next time he saddled up on-screen, it would be strictly for laughs in the Rat Pack western comedy, *Sergeants 3* (1962).

FRANK SINATRA

NOW HIS EXCITEMENT EXPLODES UNDER THE WESTERN SUN!

JOHNNY CONCHO

That smoldering
Sinatra fire
flames to new heights—
as "The Man With
the Golden Arm"
steps into
spurred
boots—
and burns
a new brand on
the screen!

"Don't run
Johnny
don't run!"

Co-starring
KEENAN   WILLIAM   PHYLLIS
WYNN · CONRAD · KIRK

Released thru UNITED ARTISTS

with
WALLACE FORD
WILLIS BOUCHEY

Screenplay by
DAVID P. HARMON
& DON McGUIRE

Based On
A Story by
DAVID P.
HARMON

Directed by
DON
McGUIRE

Produced by FRANK SINATRA · Music by NELSON RIDDLE · A KENT PRODUCTION

Neither audiences nor critics
responded to *Johnny Concho*, which
disappeared quickly from theaters.

HIGH SOCIETY

AN MGM PICTURE | 1956

Director
Charles Walters

Screenplay
John Patrick

Based on *The Philadelphia Story*
by Philip Barry

Principal Cast
Bing Crosby (C. K. Dexter-Haven), Grace Kelly (Tracy Samantha Lord), Frank Sinatra (Mike Connor), Celeste Holm (Liz Imbrie), John Lund (George Kittredge), Louis Calhern (Uncle Willie), Sidney Blackmer (Seth Lord), Louis Armstrong and his band (Themselves), Margalo Gillmore (Margaret Lord), Lydia Reed (Caroline Lord), Gordon Richards (Dexter-Haven's butler), Richard Garrick (Lord's butler)

"NO *PHILADELPHIA STORY*," wrote Bosley Crowther in the August 10, 1956 edition of the *New York Times*, unfavorably comparing *High Society* to its source material. His disdain was echoed by *Time* magazine's critic, who declared Charles Walters' film "simply not top-drawer," despite *High Society*'s starry pedigree and an impeccable score by Cole Porter.

Although some critics may have found *High Society* lacking, the public flocked to see the first pairing of Bing Crosby and Frank Sinatra onscreen. Earning $13 million-plus at the box office, *High Society* was one of the top-grossing films of 1956. And why not? They may not be Cary Grant and James Stewart, but Crosby and Sinatra shine opposite the drop-dead gorgeous Grace Kelly, who takes on Katharine Hepburn's career-resurrecting role in this musical version of the 1940 screen classic upon which *High Society* was based. Best of all, there are Cole Porter's witty songs, which Crosby and Sinatra sing with inimitable style and sophistication.

In fact, the story goes that Sinatra was sold on the role of Mike Connor, intrepid reporter for *Spy* magazine, by the chance to sing a duet with Crosby, one of his childhood idols. That duet, arguably the best number in the film, is "Well, Did You Evah?," in which Connor (Sinatra) and millionaire C. K. Dexter-Haven (Crosby) clink glasses at a

> ## "But I don't want to be worshipped. I want to be loved."

Tracy Lord (Grace Kelly)

> ## "You were extremely attractive, Tracy. And as for distant and forbidding, the contrary. However, you were somewhat a little the worse, or the better, for the wine. And there are rules about things like that."

Mike Connor (Sinatra) explains to Tracy Lord why, despite her feminine charms, all he did after their midnight swim was carry her to her room, deposit her in bed, and depart.

Left: Three forced smiles as Tracy, flanked by ex-husband Dexter-Haven (Bing Crosby) and husband-to-be George Kittredge (John Lund), poses for a photograph.

Right: Tracy takes Mike for a ride, literally and figuratively.

party for Dexter-Haven's ex-wife Tracy Lord (Kelly) on the eve of her wedding to the stodgy George Kittredge (John Lund). Cole Porter had written the song in 1939 for the Broadway musical *Du Barry Was a Lady*; with Sinatra and Crosby itching to sing to one another, it seemed the perfect time to resurrect it. With Sinatra and Crosby lending their voices to the effort, the number's delicious Porter lyrics ("Have you heard that Mimsie Starr, just got pinched in the As . . . tor bar?") never sounded so good.

There are many other terrific numbers in the film. Sinatra sings "Who Wants to Be a Millionaire?" with Celeste Holm, who plays his tough-cookie *Spy Magazine* sidekick and not-so-secret admirer. They ham it up, pooh-poohing the perks of unlimited wealth with lines like "Who wants the bother of a country estate? A country estate is something I'd hate!" Dexter-Haven croons of "True Love" to Tracy Lord during her flashback to better days; the song became a million-copy seller, earning Crosby and Kelly a platinum record. Mike Connor serenades Tracy as well, with "You're Sensational," as he too falls for her abundant charms—corny, yes, but when Sinatra puts his singular voice to work, even schmaltz goes down like fine caviar. Last, but hardly least, is "Now You Has Jazz," which showcases not only Crosby, but also Louis "Satchmo" Armstrong and his formidable band.

All in all, Cole Porter earned the $250,000 the film's producer Sol Siegel paid him; without his songs and music, you'd have to wonder what MGM was thinking. Grace Kelly was all of twenty-six when she made *High Society*, while Crosby was fifty-three. As Bosley Crowther wrote, "He [Crosby] wanders around the place like a mellow uncle, having fun with Mr. Armstrong and his boys and viewing the feminine flutter with an amiable masculine disdain. He strokes his pipe with more affection than he strokes Miss Kelly's porcelain arms."

Indeed, from a believability standpoint, *High Society* might barely rate a three—Tracy Lord is about to marry a prig she doesn't love in order to spite her ex, Dexter-Haven, whom she still loves, and who still loves her; in the meantime, she falls for reporter Mike Connor, who has

Together at last on-screen—Sinatra and Crosby perform "Well, Did You Evah?"

"Have you heard? It's in the stars, next July we collide with Mars."

From the Cole Porter song "Well, Did You Evah?," sung by C. K. Dexter-Haven (Bing Crosby) and Mike Connor as they share a drink together at Uncle Willie's hideaway bar.

yet to realize he really loves his co-reporter Liz Imbrie, who in turn secretly loves him. One gets the sense that when all is said and done, there are uncontrollable passions lurking even among the ultra rich, but all must be resolved in the most conventional of ways. This was probably true in 1939, when playwright Philip Barry wrote the original play for Hepburn, but somehow the application of Vistacolor and 1950s morality seems to throw a wet towel on much of the visceral spontaneity present in the 1940 film.

Perhaps Sinatra, in the role that won James Stewart an Academy Award in 1940, deserves some of the blame. While praising the star's vocal stylings in *High Society*, Crowther observed that "Sinatra plays the reporter like a dead-end kid with a typewriter." Still, when he opens his mouth to sing, it's easy to forget all that and just be thankful that Louis B. Mayer famously insisted messages were for Western Union, so that his studio could crank out escapist fare as polished and elegant as *High Society*.

Above: Mike carries Tracy back to the house after their late-night dip in Uncle Willie's pool.

Left: The great Louis "Satchmo" Armstrong blows his trumpet during the lively "Now You Has Jazz" number. And why does a film based on *The Philadelphia Story* take place in Newport, Rhode Island? MGM was then developing a film based on several *New Yorker* magazine articles by Lillian Ross about the Newport Jazz Festival, so why not combine that project with this tale of romantic hijinks among the mega-moneyed?

Opposite top: Dexter-Haven consoles a dazed Mike by explaining, "I thought I better hit you before he did—he's in much better shape than I am."

Opposite bottom: Some quick thinking is in order as Tracy, her parents (Margalo Gillmore and Sidney Blackmer), Dexter-Haven, Liz, and Mike prepare to face a room full of wedding guests.

Above: Tracy and Mike finally lock lips by the swimming pool.

THE PRIDE AND THE PASSION

A UNITED ARTISTS RELEASE | 1957

Director

Stanley Kramer

Screenplay

Edna and Edward Anhalt

Based on the novel *The Gun* by
C. S. Forester

Principal Cast

Cary Grant (Anthony Trumbull),
Frank Sinatra (Miguel),
Sophia Loren (Juana), Theodore
Bikel (General Jouvet),
John Wengraf (Sermaine), Jay
Novello (Ballinger)

FRANK SINATRA'S recording work in the mid–1950s was the most creative and daring of his career, and resulted in one hit album after another. But on film, where he had less control over the finished product, results were mixed. The public loved to see and hear him sing in the movies, but making musicals was too easy; Sinatra liked a challenge. He wanted to push himself artistically, and in 1956 that meant taking on a role and a film vastly different from anything he'd done before. He signed on to work with producer/director Stanley Kramer, and flew to Spain for four months' work on *The Pride and the Passion*.

Set in the Spanish countryside circa 1810, *The Pride and the Passion* is an epic drama about the masses uniting to take back their homeland from Napoleon's marauding forces. At the center of the story is a massive seven-ton cannon, abandoned by Spanish troops fleeing the French army, and retrieved by a band of rebel Spaniards determined to put it to use at any cost. Leading the charge with thousands behind him is Spanish peasant Miguel (Frank Sinatra) aided by his girlfriend Juana (Sophia Loren), and joined by British naval captain Anthony Trumbull (Cary Grant).

Although Trumbull would prefer to bring the cannon back to England, he agrees to stay on and share his weapons expertise with the rebels.

> **"I am Miguel of the gun and of Avila."**
>
> ....
>
> **Miguel (Sinatra) to a bullfight crowd**

> **"I do not know history, but I do know this. That I will stand before the statue of Santa Teresa in Avila."**
>
> ....
>
> **Miguel to Anthony Trumbull (Cary Grant)**

> **"I do not ask you to die or even to bleed. Just to sweat a little."**
>
> ....
>
> **Miguel to a crowd of Spanish peasants**

Left: Juana (Sophia Loren) is moved by the music in a Spanish courtyard.

Right: Miguel, the rebel leader, clashes with naval captain Anthony Trumbull, but enlists him to repair the rebels' seven-ton cannon.

When Juana and Trumbull fall in love, Miguel is unfazed; thick-skinned and single-minded in his mission, he accepts the turn of events as yet another cruelty of war. As they march toward the Spanish walled city of Avila, determined to drive off the occupying forces, the weapon becomes a symbol of power and control, and a rallying point for the rebel troops who follow Miguel into battle at the wave of an arm. The French army wants the cannon as well, so the rebels are tested in a series of exciting confrontations before they've even had a chance to see what the incredible weapon can do.

The three lead actors in *The Pride and the Passion* deliver excellent performances, but they are clearly challenging themselves with roles quite different from what their fans had come to expect. Cary Grant, in his third decade as a film icon, was enjoying enormous popularity as a middle-aged romantic lead, and his choice of roles was key; his characters in *To Catch a Thief* (1955) and *An Affair to Remember* (1957) showcased his uncanny skills with witty banter, and his well-cultivated image as a good-natured sophisticate. *The Pride and the Passion*, however, had no clever dialogue for Grant and his character acts annoyed and frustrated a good deal of the time. Likewise, the acting skills of Sophia Loren, so powerful in *The Gold of Naples* (1954), were greatly under-utilized in a role that had her mostly standing by silently, save for her most prominent scene—an erotic dance in which she stomps and shimmies while the men stare in awe. As for Sinatra, it requires a huge suspension of disbelief to accept him as a Spanish peasant. Of course, during Hollywood's golden age, Caucasian actors regularly donned wigs, dark contact lenses, and heavy make-up to play ethnic roles, which often perpetuated egregious racial stereotypes. Despite his ill-fitting black wig, Sinatra gives an intense performance as Miguel, but the script leaves little room for his cinematic trademark—the twinkle in his eye.

Cary Grant and Sophia Loren were focused on each other during filming, and their off-screen romance added fire to many of their scenes. But Sinatra was focused on a relationship that had been going badly for years, and was now going tragically off-track. His tumultuous marriage to

Miguel enters the bullring, urging every Spaniard to join his cause.

Top: Juana convinces Miguel that he must bring Trumbull along, despite their differences.

Center: Trumbull and Miguel plan their attack on the French troops.

Bottom: Trumbull, Juana, and Miguel discuss a plan for floating the cannon across a river.

Top: Cary Grant and Sophia Loren had a sizzling affair during the filming of *The Pride and the Passion*.

Center: Frank Sinatra insisted on doing action scenes normally assigned to professional stunt men.

Bottom: The cannon is eased down a hillside by a legion of rebels.

Ava Gardner was rockier than ever during the shooting of *The Pride and the Passion*, and Sinatra's impatience with the filmmaking process was at an all-time high. The production was shooting in rural locations with accommodations nearby, but he insisted on staying at a luxury hotel in Madrid, a three-hour drive away. Despite the relative comfort of his suite, and a brief visit from Gardner, Sinatra was anxious to get out of Spain, and finally informed Kramer that he would not stick around for the sixteen weeks of shooting, as previously agreed. Kramer had a massive project on his hands, an astounding logistical feat involving more than 9,000 extras and a production budget of $4 million, but suddenly his biggest problem was Sinatra. Kramer saved the film by rearranging the shooting schedule and filming Sinatra's scenes first, and later filming other Sinatra scenes on a Los Angeles soundstage.

Trouble behind the scenes did not prevent *The Pride and the Passion* from becoming a box-office success when it opened in July 1957, buoyed by the fact that Sinatra was once again an enormously popular recording artist and firmly established as the cool singer for adults—or for anyone who wasn't interested in getting "all shook up." In the *Saturday Review* Hollis Alpert wrote, "While the gun deserves a special Academy Award, Mr. Sinatra must be commended for his restrained and appealing *guerillero* leader." *Variety* gave Sinatra credit for being "more colorful" than his talented co-stars, and wrote that "he looks and behaves like a Spanish rebel leader, earthy and cruel and skilled in handling his men in the primitive warfare. His is a splendid performance."

More than a decade later, in one of his TV specials, Sinatra spoofed his performance as Miguel in *The Pride and the Passion*. But if he ultimately considered the role a poor fit, his fans largely disagreed. Sinatra had passed the point where he was expected to be the charming crooner onscreen; he had range, and the public knew it. Creatively Sinatra was on a journey, and his audience was with him no matter what bumps lay in the road.

THE JOKER IS WILD

A PARAMOUNT PICTURE | 1957

Director
Charles Vidor

Screenplay
Oscar Saul

Based on the book *The Life of Joe E. Lewis* by Art Cohn

Principal Cast
Frank Sinatra (Joe E. Lewis), Mitzi Gaynor (Martha Stewart), Jeanne Crain (Letty Page), Eddie Albert (Austin Mack), Beverly Garland (Cassie Mack), Jackie Coogan (Swifty Morgan), Barry Kelley (Captain McCarthy), Ted de Corsia (George Parker), Leonard Graves (Tim Coogan)

A BONA-FIDE passion project for Sinatra, *The Joker Is Wild* is probably best remembered today for introducing one of the star's signature songs, the Academy Award–winning "All the Way" by Jimmy Van Heusen and Sammy Cahn. However, this compelling yet uneven chronicle of the life and times of entertainer Joe E. Lewis deserves reappraisal as one of the finest showcases of Sinatra's dramatic range; he gives one of his most vivid and nuanced performances as Lewis, who survived a brutal attack by Chicago mobsters to reinvent himself as a successful nightclub comic.

Although Lewis is somewhat forgotten today, he was one of Sinatra's idols. In fact, Sinatra was so eager to bring Lewis' colorful life to the screen that he bought the rights to Art Cohn's 1955 biography of the star and brokered a deal with Paramount Pictures to produce and distribute *The Joker Is Wild*.

Adapted for the screen by Oscar Saul, who had previously collaborated with Tennessee Williams on the film version of *A Streetcar Named Desire* (1951), *The Joker Is Wild* begins in '20s-era Chicago, where Lewis (Sinatra) is the star attraction at a nightclub run by gangster Tim Coogan (Leonard Graves). Ignoring the advice of his friend and accompanist Austin Mack (Eddie Albert), Lewis incurs the wrath of Coogan by taking a higher-paying gig in another nightclub. It's a reckless decision that will

"I got a right to work anyplace I want to."

Joe E. Lewis (Sinatra)

"In the glare of the spotlight the heart of an entertainer is candidly revealed."

The Joker Is Wild trailer

"You had more fun playing my life than I had living it"

Joe E. Lewis to Sinatra

Left: Sinatra gives one of his finest performances as Joe E. Lewis in *The Joker Is Wild*.

Right: A publicity still of Sinatra and co-star Mitzi Gaynor.

nearly cost Lewis his life, for Coogan will retaliate by slashing the singer's vocal cords and beating him unconscious.

No longer able to sing, Lewis leaves Chicago for New York City, where he ekes out a marginal living as a burlesque clown. Humiliated and despondent, Lewis turns increasingly to alcohol to dull his pain, even as his career heats up and he finds love with a beautiful socialite, Letty Page (Jeanne Crain). She seemingly represents everything he wants, but Lewis ultimately drives her away, only to sink further into alcoholic bitterness. He subsequently marries showgirl Martha Stewart (Mitzi Gaynor in a rare dramatic role), yet their union is strained from the start, due to his drinking and the respective demands of their show business careers. Finally, after he's lost nearly everything, Lewis realizes that he must quit drinking to find happiness.

The sole biopic in Sinatra's filmography, *The Joker Is Wild* doesn't break any new dramatic ground in its portrait of a tortured showbiz personality stumbling towards redemption. Nor does it skirt one of the narrative pitfalls of the biopic genre, i.e., the episodic "and then this happened" approach to storytelling that characterizes even the finest examples of the genre, like *Coal Miner's Daughter* (1979) and *Ray* (2004). This is particularly apparent in the film's second, arguably weaker half, depicting Lewis's downward spiral into booze and self-pity. These shortcomings aside, *The Joker Is Wild* is a handsomely mounted and emotionally involving film, skillfully directed by veteran Charles Vidor, whose credits included *Gilda* (1946) and the Ruth Etting biopic, *Love Me or Leave Me* (1955). Personally chosen by Sinatra to helm *The Joker Is Wild*, Vidor ably guides Sinatra in the difficult role of Lewis: the star captures the wounded vulnerability, resilient wit, and selfishness of Lewis, a cocky, larger-than-life personality who occasionally acts like a self-absorbed jerk. It's a beautifully modulated performance capped by Sinatra's iconic rendition of "All the Way."

Above: Starting over at the bottom, Lewis swallows his pride to work as a burlesque clown in New York City.

Opposite: Jeanne Crain as Letty Page, the beautiful socialite Lewis drives away.

PAL JOEY

A COLUMBIA PICTURE | 1957

Director

George Sidney

Screenwriter

Dorothy Kingsley

Based on the play by John O'Hara

Principal Cast

Frank Sinatra (Joey Evans), Rita Hayworth (Vera Simpson), Kim Novak (Linda English), Barbara Nichols (Gladys), Bobby Sherwood (Ned Galvin), Hank Henry (Mike Miggins)

NASTY, RUDE, inconsiderate, uncooperative, and ungrateful," but also "quietly generous and considerate without even expecting thanks," wrote *Los Angeles Mirror News* reporter Kendis Rocklin of Frank Sinatra in a mid-1950s profile. In other words, the mercurial star was perfect casting for the titular *Pal Joey*. Considerably softened from his origins in a series of *New Yorker* stories and the hit 1940 Broadway musical that made Sinatra's friend Gene Kelly a star, this Joey Evans is devil and angel, a heel who is all heart, and a role Sinatra could wear like a well-tailored suit.

A dancer in his original Broadway incarnation, Joey became a singer in George Sidney's film version in a move befitting its leading man's platinum pipes. Sinatra's Joey Evans isn't a has-been; he's a never-was, all id and ferocious ambition. A one-way ticket from a police force eager to be rid of him brings Joey to San Francisco. He lands a gig as an emcee/singer at a Barbary Coast nightclub where he quickly becomes the cheese that most of the "mice" (Joey's slang for chorus girls) crave. When he meets society matron—and former stripper—Vera Simpson (Rita Hayworth, three years younger than Sinatra, playing the "older" woman) Joey sees her as his proverbial meal ticket. Even though he may be falling for Linda English (Sinatra's *Man with the Golden Arm* costar Kim

> "**Drunks tossing pennies, that's the story of my life, but I'm going places. One of these days, I'm going to have a club of my very own, my name up in lights, no hokey waiters rattling plates while I'm on, no tough managers belting me around. I'll be my own boss. Nobody owns Joey but Joey.**"
>
> Joey Evans (Sinatra)

> "**We're alike, Joey and I, the same breed of cat.**"
>
> Vera Simpson (Rita Hayworth)

Joey baits the hook in his campaign to seduce Linda (Kim Novak) as they dance.

Novak), a mouse seemingly immune to his rakish charm, the avowedly independent Joey becomes Vera's gigolo as a means of getting what he ultimately wants: his own nightclub.

In the 1940s, Columbia head Harry Cohn nearly made *Pal Joey* with Kelly reprising his Broadway turn opposite his *Cover Girl* costar Hayworth (in the role of Linda English), but MGM thwarted his plans when the studio demanded too high a price for Kelly's services in a loan-out deal. Plans to cast either James Cagney or Cary Grant in the role also came to nothing. When the studio revived the project in the 1950s, it was supposed to be a vehicle for Marlon Brando and Mae West with Billy Wilder directing. That, too, fell through.

The movie finally came to fruition when Sinatra's production company, Essex, formed a partnership with director George Sidney and producer Fred Kohlmar. Screenwriter Dorothy Kingsley, an Oscar nominee for *Seven Brides for Seven Brothers* (1954), was responsible for the Production Code-mandated softening of the hard-edged character that author John O'Hara had created and honed through his stories and the musical. There were other changes, as well. The play's female newspaper reporter, who sang "Zip" in the play, was jettisoned. The number, an ode

Top: Joey watches Vera with delight as she performs a demure version of her old burlesque routine.

Center: "That's why the lady is a tramp," Joey sings to solo customer Vera in a bid to breach her defenses.

Bottom: Joey prepares to go to Vera, while a hurt Linda watches.

to striptease, now belonged to Vera, providing Hayworth with an opportunity to pay homage to her notorious "Put the Blame on Mame" number from *Gilda* (1946). Only ten of Richard Rodgers and Lorenz Hart's fourteen songs from the musical made it into the film, with four other tunes from the songwriters' extensive catalog added to the mix. The most significant of the new additions is "The Lady is a Tramp"; Sinatra's soulful rendering of this song is one of the undeniable highlights of *Pal Joey*.

The year 1957 was a tough one for Sinatra. In January, he fell into a deep depression when his close friend Humphrey Bogart succumbed to lung cancer. He had legal troubles on two fronts. A California State Senate Committee subpoenaed him as it investigated his involvement in a 1954 raid on the home of a woman that pal Joe DiMaggio thought was his wife Marilyn Monroe's lover. He was also in a legal battle with *Look* magazine, which he sued for libel after an unflattering profile appeared in the magazine's pages. Then a week before *Pal Joey*'s October 25 premiere, his new TV variety show, *The Frank Sinatra Show*, debuted on ABC to poor reviews and dismal ratings.

Outside troubles did not seem to bother him on the *Pal Joey* set, according to the director. "Sinatra and I, my God, we got on wonderfully," Sidney remembered four decades later. "We had great times together. When he came in, he had complete concentration. When he's in that scene, you could shoot a gun off, he wouldn't hear it." The equanimity Sinatra displayed on set extended to his generous attitude toward billing. With three stars to mollify, Columbia bosses dithered, unsure how to broach the touchy subject. Sinatra brought it up first, saying, "What's the trouble? If it's billing, it's okay to make it Hayworth/Sinatra/Novak, I don't mind being in the middle of that sandwich."

When he was asked if he'd seen the movie, *Pal Joey* creator John O'Hara quipped, "No, I don't have to see Sinatra. I invented him." Critics agreed: this was a role Sinatra was born to inhabit. Many of the reviews quibbled about the bowdlerization of the play in its transition to the screen with *Look* magazine describing the film adaptation as "watered down" and *Time* calling it "oversanitized." But *Time* added, "The show is

> **"I know all about you. I don't want you sniffing around the customers' dames. One false move and you're out on your Francis."**
>
> Barbary Coast manager Mike Miggins (Hank Henry) laying down the law to his new emcee Joey Evans

Above: A love triangle comes to life as Joey imagines himself tripping the light fantastic onstage with Linda and Vera.

Opposite: Linda smolders as she sings "My Funny Valentine" in the solo spotlight.

"Some guys got a system with horses. I got a system with dames. You treat a dame like a lady and treat a lady like a dame."

Joey Evans explains his approach to seduction

saved by Frank Sinatra, who does a tremendous job in the title role. Pal Joey was a hoofer in the play, and Sinatra does not dance a step in the film, but somehow he crowds the screen with rhythm every time he moves." *Look* was equally impressed, writing, "Frank Sinatra plays Joey with all the brass the role demands . . . He tosses off both dames and songs with equal artistry, and almost single-handedly makes *Pal Joey* a wonderfully entertaining movie."

"Potent" is how *Variety* described his turn, while A. H. Weiler in the *New York Times* raved, " There is no doubt that this is largely Mr. Sinatra's show. As the amiable grifter with an iron ego, he projects a distinctly bouncy, likable personality into an unusual role."

The laurels did not end with those raves. Though the Academy overlooked him at Oscar time, Sinatra won the Golden Globe for Best Actor in a Musical or Comedy and a Laurel Award for Top Male Musical Performance. The movie went on to make $4.7 million at the box office, while the soundtrack album rose to number two on the Billboard charts. The year 1957 might have given Sinatra a rough ride, but *Pal Joey* brought it to a close with one of his greatest triumphs.

KINGS GO FORTH

A UNITED ARTISTS RELEASE | 1958

Director
Delmer Daves

Screenplay
Merle Miller

Based on the novel by Joe
David Brown

Principal Cast
Frank Sinatra (1st Lt. Sam
Loggins), Tony Curtis (Cpl. Britt
Harris), Natalie Wood (Monique
Blair), Leora Dana (Mrs. Blair),
Karl Swenson (the Colonel),
Edward Ryder (Cpl. Lindsay),
Ann Codee (Mme. Brieux)

FRANK SINATRA NEVER trod the boards on Broadway as an actor, but he came close with his riveting performance in *Kings Go Forth*, a drama based on a novel but largely filmed like a play. The film requires Sinatra to deliver a performance both heart-wrenching and understated, filmed in a style that allowed him to stretch as an actor and let his facial expressions and body language tell the tale. Filmed largely in close-up, with long, uncut shots, Sinatra's job is to carry the film by delivering dialogue, and the silences in between, in a fascinating way.

Kings Go Forth is a World War II-era story set in the south of France, where American GIs continued to fight German forces in the mountains just a few hours' drive from the bustling French Riviera. Sinatra plays 1st Lt. Sam Loggins, who leads his men through dangerous missions during the week, then spends his weekends in Nice, a convenient playground for the U.S. military with its cafés, nightclubs, and gorgeous oceanfront scenery. On one such retreat Loggins meets young Monique Blair (Natalie Wood), an American raised in France, and finds her innocence and charm impossible to resist. Soon he is courting her, and rushing into Nice every chance he gets to spend time with her, happily whiling away the hours in the opulent home she shares with her mother (Leora Dana). But Monique ends the affair abruptly, telling Loggins that she knows how Americans feel

> "In America some people just don't wait. They feel like kissing, they kiss. Kiss, kiss, kiss, all the time. That's how I feel with you."

Lt. Sam Loggins (Sinatra) to Monique Blair (Natalie Wood)

Left: Lt. Sam Loggins checks papers on Cpl. Britt Harris (Tony Curtis), a new arrival who is soon to become his friend and rival.

Right: Sinatra discusses the film's literary origins in the *Kings Go Forth* theatrical trailer.

> "I'm not much of a catch. Matter of fact, nobody ever tried to catch me. And I've never tried to catch anybody either."

Lt. Sam Loggins to Monique Blair

Above: Loggins leads his men on a reconnaissance mission.

Left: Loggins is enchanted by Monique (Natalie Wood).

After a daring move that saved his platoon, Harris rests while Loggins offers his gratitude.

about people like her: She's of mixed race, she says, with a white mother and an African-American father.

Back on duty, Loggins wrestles with his feelings for Monique and his prejudices, and tries to be a leader for a group of GIs that includes a rambunctious new corporal named Britt Harris (Tony Curtis), a wealthy playboy determined to win a few medals while sampling the local beauties. Harris sets his sights on Monique, and quickly sweeps her away from Loggins. Loggins backs off, but reminds Harris not to play with Monique's heart, an admonishment that begins as a friendly warning and quickly escalates to threats. Just as Loggins' anger with Harris reaches its peak, he learns that he'll be leading Harris on a dangerous two-man mission, where the rivals will be forced to depend on each other for their lives.

Combat action in *Kings Go Forth* is spectacular, with rear-projection scenes at a minimum and a good deal of dirt flying in the real French Alpes-Maritimes. The two-man mission with Curtis and Sinatra is paced for excitement, and the result is at least as suspenseful as scenes in more celebrated fare of the time, such as *North by Northwest* (1959). But *Kings Go Forth* is more a parlor drama than an action film, with many quiet, dialogue-driven moments as compelling as any of the combat sequences. In long, intimate scenes the characters act and react in real time, often giving *Kings Go Forth* the distinct feeling of a stage play. It's a visually rewarding

"Everyone in the world has some kind of a burden. But it is not the burden that's important. It's how you carry it."

Monique Blair to Lt. Sam Loggins

Monique shows Loggins the piece of bread she keeps as a reminder of her family's past struggles.

"I've seen you in action, comrade, and I just wanted you to know that Monique is a very nice girl and she bruises easily. I know."

Lt. Sam Loggins to Cpl. Britt Harris (Tony Curtis)

film as well, thanks to cinematographer Daniel L. Fapp's beautifully composed black and white images.

The Civil Rights Era in America had begun, but issues of race were still daring subject matter for films when *Kings Go Forth* came out in 1958. Sinatra embraced the issue, however, as he had throughout his career. In the mid-1940s, when every jukebox in the nation was playing his hits, he used his celebrity to speak out against racial hatred, even delivering speeches in communities where racial tensions ran high. From the lectern, and in his interviews, Sinatra made it clear that racial equality was one of the issues he cared about most, and that he intended to continue speaking about it publicly for the rest of his life. On this issue producer Frank Ross agreed with Sinatra wholeheartedly, and their shared sensibility is what brought them together to work on *Kings Go Forth*. It was a reunion of sorts; thirteen years earlier, Ross and Sinatra had teamed up to create the short film, *The House I Live In*, a lesson on religious tolerance that had earned Sinatra an Honorary Academy Award in 1946.

As a recording artist Sinatra soared in 1958, releasing two of the biggest-selling albums of his career, *Come Fly with Me* and *Frank Sinatra Sings for Only the Lonely*. In between those landmark "theme" albums he also released a string of hit singles, including the tune "Monique," created to promote the June release of *Kings Go Forth,* though the song is never actually performed onscreen. In 1958 Sinatra was also the star of his own television program, and a favorite subject for scores of fan magazines. His fans made *Kings Go Forth* a hit, even as critics continued to grapple with the fact that Sinatra could be astounding on both disk and the screen. "The Thin Singer has never had a more difficult role and he has never more completely mastered a characterization," wrote Dorothy Manners in the *Los Angeles Examiner.* "Might as well admit it, he's a great actor."

Between concert dates, television, records, and films, Sinatra in 1958 was a creative powerhouse, showing no sign that he intended to slow down. Of the two films he made that year, *Some Came Running* may have garnered more attention, but *Kings Go Forth* is a subtle and powerful drama that features one of Sinatra's most beautifully modulated performances.

Top: Loggins watches as Harris and Monique fall in love.

Center: Harris assures Loggins that his feelings for Monique are real.

Bottom: Despite their rivalry in love, Loggins and Harris work as a team during a dangerous combat operation.

SOME CAME RUNNING

AN MGM PICTURE | 1958

Director
Vincente Minnelli

Screenplay
John Patrick and Arthur
Sheekman

Based on the novel by
James Jones

Principal Cast
Frank Sinatra (Dave Hirsh), Dean
Martin (Bama Dillert), Shirley
MacLaine (Ginny Moorehead),
Martha Hyer (Gwen French),
Arthur Kennedy (Frank Hirsh),
Nancy Gates (Edith Barclay),
Leora Dana (Agnes Hirsh), Betty
Lou Keim (Dawn Hirsh)

WHEN NOVELIST James Jones finished *Some Came Running*, his follow-up to *From Here to Eternity*, MGM was eager to acquire the rights. Hoping to recapture the success of Jones' prior work, MGM bought the film rights to *Some Came Running* and signed Sinatra to star. Screenwriters John Patrick and Arthur Sheekman took the 1,266-page tome and streamlined the plot, but it remains a collage of several narrative threads, characters, and themes depicting the demands of society, love, and hypocrisy.

Shot in the small town of Madison, Indiana, *Some Came Running* begins with Dave Hirsh (Frank Sinatra) waking up in a Greyhound bus hung over and chagrined that he has arrived in his hometown of Parkman, Indiana, a place he hasn't seen in sixteen years. Dave realizes that he must have mentioned the town to his drinking buddies in Chicago. They not only bought him a ticket, but sent a call girl, Ginny Moorhead (Shirley MacLaine), to accompany him.

While Ginny is thrilled to be with him, Dave gives her some money and tells her to go home. After she slinks away, Dave makes his way to a local hotel. He settles in with a bottle of whiskey and asks a clerk to make a deposit for him at a local bank.

In short order, Frank (Arthur Kennedy), Dave's social-climbing brother, comes calling. He tries to keep it friendly, but he's irked that several people

"Dawn, honey, bumming around can only help make you a bum."

Dave Hirsh (Sinatra)

"Man, you sure don't look pretty this morning, Dave. Wow."

Bama Dillert (Dean Martin)

"You're right, Teacher. You're 100% right. I've been a bad boy. I've been naughty. Matter of fact I don't even belong in your class."

Dave Hirsh to Gwen French (Martha Hyer)

Left: Dave listens intently to Gwen French, a creative writing instructor.

Right: Arriving in his hometown, Dave explains to Ginny (Shirley MacLaine) that it's time to go their separate ways.

heard that Dave was back in town before he did. Warily, Frank asks Dave, now that he's out of the army, what his plans are. Dave is non-committal, but says he will not be pursuing his writing, even though he has two published novels. Frank glosses over their mutual discomfort and invites Dave to dinner.

That night, Dave is pleased to meet his niece, Dawn (Betty Lou Keim), but he is more intrigued by Gwen French (Martha Hyer), the beautiful creative writing instructor. She is drawn to him by his writing talent, but is unnerved by his attentions. Winding up alone, Dave ends the night at the local bar where he runs into Ginny again and plays cards with Bama Dillert (Dean Martin), a traveling gambler. As the days pass, Dave falls hard for Gwen, joins forces with Bama, and begins a friendship of convenience with Ginny. His exploits embarrass Frank and frighten Gwen. When Dave discovers the hypocrisy of Frank's life and Gwen's true feelings, he deals with his disappointment in unexpected ways.

Apparently, Sinatra shared his character's disdain for small-town life. While shooting in Madison, Sinatra was reportedly rude to the locals. He also had run-ins with his accomplished director, Vincente Minnelli. Minnelli's deliberate and detail-oriented approach to filmmaking was anathema to the high-strung Sinatra. The breaking point came when Minnelli wanted to move a Ferris wheel instead of the camera to achieve the perfect shot. It was a change that would require massive delays and send an outraged Sinatra hopping a plane back to Los Angeles with his buddy, Dean Martin. Only after the producer, Sol Siegel, persuaded him to reconsider did Sinatra and Martin return to the set.

Later, when shooting interior shots back in Los Angeles, Sinatra argued for moving the usual 7AM starting time to noon. "Performers work better in the afternoon and the girls look better. They don't run out of gas at five like they usually do." Minnelli bowed to Sinatra's wishes.

Sinatra got along much better with his friend, Dean Martin. Before *Some Came Running*, Martin was struggling to establish himself as a solo artist after his split with his partner, Jerry Lewis. Sinatra gave Martin the opportunity to do just that by having him cast as Bama Dillert in *Some Came Running*. Martin is convincing as a charming gambler, but his continual referral to

Opposite top: Bama Dillert (Dean Martin) invites Dave to a card game.

Opposite center: Dave sees his brother, Frank Hirsh (Arthur Kennedy), for the first time in sixteen years.

Opposite bottom: At the local bar, Dave runs into Ginny and her jealous escort, Raymond (Steven Peck).

"And this is Dave Hirsh who returned to shake loose the sins, the shame, the secrets of an entire town so that it would never be the same."

Trailer for *Some Came Running*

Dave and Gwen confront the differences between them.

women as "pigs" is jolting. Martin and Sinatra have an easy rapport onscreen that is especially evident in the poker game scenes. At one point in the action, Sinatra smiles (a rare gesture in this film) and says, "Ain't that a kick in the head?" Martin reacts with a barely held-in laugh. That phrase would appear again in 1960 as the title of a song on the soundtrack of Sinatra's film *Ocean's Eleven* (1960) and as a hit on the charts for Dean Martin.

Sinatra didn't know Shirley MacLaine when he first spotted her in a television special and suggested her for the part of Ginny, but they developed a friendship. While on location, MacLaine stayed in a hotel next to a house that was rented for Martin and Sinatra. According to MacLaine, Sinatra and Martin routinely played cards all night with a revolving group of visiting "friends" and mob associates: "That's where I met Sam Giancana." Sinatra helped out his new friend by suggesting a change in the screenplay that he felt would garner MacLaine an Academy Award nomination for Best Actress. Per his request, the fatal scene that ends the book was changed in the final film version. The result was that MacLaine was indeed later nominated for an Academy Award and a Golden Globe.

Critical reaction was mixed for *Some Came Running*. Bosley Crowther of the *New York Times* said, "It is all very complex and confused." However, he found Sinatra "downright fascinating." *Variety* said, "The story is pure melodrama . . . Sinatra gives a top performance, sardonic and compassionate, full of touches instinctive and technical." Commercially, the film did well and in pop culture annals it is remembered as the precursor to the "Rat Pack" films that featured Sinatra's core group of friends.

Shirley MacLaine was not the only one in the film who was nominated for an Academy Award. Arthur Kennedy was nominated for Best Supporting Actor and Martha Hyer was nominated for Best Supporting Actress. The film also received nominations for Best Costume Design and Best Song. None of these nominations yielded awards, but at this same ceremony, Vincente Minnelli won the award for Best Director, for *Gigi* (1958). As Minnelli's demanding *Some Came Running* star might have quipped, "Ain't that a kick in the head?"

Top: Dave joins the action in Bama's back-room poker game.

Center: Bama's date, Rosalie (Carmen Phillips), Dave, Ginny, and Bama get to know each other over a few drinks.

Bottom: MacLaine received her first Academy Award nomination for *Some Came Running*.

A HOLE IN THE HEAD

A UNITED ARTISTS RELEASE | 1959

Director

Frank Capra

Screenplay

Arnold Schulman, based on his play

Principal Cast

Frank Sinatra (Tony Manetta), Edward G. Robinson (Mario Manetta), Eleanor Parker (Mrs. Eloise Rogers), Carolyn Jones (Shirl), Thelma Ritter (Sophie Manetta), Keenan Wynn (Jerry Marks), Eddie Hodges (Ally Manetta)

A HOLE IN THE HEAD marked the return to the screen of legendary filmmaker Frank Capra. After an eight-year absence from Hollywood, the Academy Award-winning director of such classics as *It Happened One Night* (1934), *Mr. Smith Goes to Washington* (1939), and *It's a Wonderful Life* (1946) signed on as both producer and director of this Frank Sinatra vehicle. Although Capra had an impressive resume, he had to acknowledge the clout that the wildly successful Sinatra had acquired by 1959. The terms of Sincap, the production company that Sinatra and Capra created, dictated that each had an equal say in all pertinent matters, but that Sinatra would own two-thirds of the film while Capra would claim only one-third. Star power trumped directorial reputation.

Playwright Arnold Schulman adapted his 1957 Broadway play for the screen, albeit with some misgivings. He was reportedly not pleased that the play's Jewish characters became Italian-Americans in the film version, but he dutifully made the change in his screenplay. Frank Sinatra plays Tony Manetta, a free-wheeling kind of man who lives for today and doesn't worry too much about tomorrow. He's facing eviction from the Miami Beach hotel he runs, he's seeing a beatnik girl, Shirl, (Carolyn Jones) who doesn't want to be tied down, and he's raising his pre-teen son, Ally (Eddie Hodges), on hot dogs. Tony has a dream to build a Disneyland

> "I'll tell you who lives on Easy Street—nobody. You want to make a million overnight. Well, it don't happen that way."

Mario (Edward G. Robinson)

Left: Tony helps his girlfriend, Shirl (Carolyn Jones) navigate the stairs.

Right: Tony shares his big dreams with his son, Ally (Eddie Hodges).

> "You've got it (imagination) and you're poor."
>
> "No, no, no. Broke many times, but never poor. You would never understand that."

Tony (Sinatra) explains himself to brother Mario

in Miami, (the film predates Disney World in Orlando) but he first needs to make sure he won't be evicted.

Desperate, Tony makes a call to his hardworking, humorless brother, Mario (Edward G. Robinson), asking for help. Mario flies down from New York with his sweet but worried wife, Sophie (Thelma Ritter). They recognize that Tony, a widower, and Ally have a great relationship, but want to bring Ally back to New York to give him a proper childhood. Tony is angered by this proposal and tells them that he just needs a few thousand dollars to get back on his feet. Mario and Sophie tell him that if he got married and settled down they would be more inclined to help him. To that end, Tony agrees to meet Mrs. Rogers (Eleanor Parker), a local widow Sophie knows. Tony and Mrs. Rogers spend a lovely evening together and their prospects look good. However, when Tony's wealthy old buddy Jerry Marks (Keenan Wynn) comes to town, the lure of easy money pulls Tony back into his irresponsible ways. Within the span of just one night, Tony risks everything he holds dear.

As was his modus operandi during filming, Sinatra made clear that he wanted to do only one take per scene. He felt he gave a more natural and spontaneous performance that way, and he had little patience for the rehearsal process. In contrast, screen veteran Edward G. Robinson wanted to rehearse thoroughly because he became progressively better with each pass. In his defense, Sinatra reportedly told Robinson, "I don't believe in exhausting myself before the take. On the other hand, I read the script fifty times before I ever go to work. So you can't say I'm unprepared." Capra's solution was to repeatedly rehearse Robinson with a stand-in until Robinson was ready to do the scene with one-take Sinatra.

The final film displays a contrast in performance styles as well. Robinson gives a somewhat one-dimensional portrayal of the disapproving brother. He is not helped by a script that has him criticizing Sinatra's character in a similar manner time and time again. Sinatra's performance is more nuanced and natural. Although his character is always playing the angles, he never seems truly devious. Sinatra manages to reveal the basi-

Top: Carolyn Jones steals scenes as the free-spirited Shirl.

Center: Mario (Edward G. Robinson) and Sophie (Thelma Ritter) anxiously take a call from Tony while son Julius (Jimmy Komack) listens.

Bottom: Tony tries to cheer up Ally.

Top: Mrs. Rogers (Eleanor Parker) makes small talk with Tony's family.

Center: Tony and Mrs. Rogers share a moment alone.

Bottom: Tony comes to realize what his actions have cost him.

cally good essence of a man who seems incapable of doing what responsible society expects of him. This dynamic is best displayed in the scenes between Sinatra's character and his son, played by Hodges. Although Tony cannot provide a stable home or a good example of responsible living to his son, there is no question that he not only cares deeply for Ally, but sincerely enjoys his company.

While Robinson does little with his role as the family scold, character actress par excellence Thelma Ritter brings warmth and a depth of feeling to her character of Sophie, who could have easily been played as an anxious worrywart. Carolyn Jones radiates breezy good cheer as the beatnik and Keenan Wynn plays Jerry with the appropriate mixture of bluster and menace.

A Hole in the Head enjoyed both commercial and critical success. One of 1959's top grossing films, it also made the *New York Times'* list of the year's ten best films. Calling *A Hole in the Head* "a perfect entertainment," the *New York Times'* Bosley Crowther was no less enthusiastic about the film's star: "But the prize goes to Mr. Sinatra, who makes the hero of this vibrant color film a softhearted, hardboiled, white-souled sheep whom we will cherish, along with Mr. Deeds and Mr. Smith, as one of the great guys that Mr. Capra has escorted to the American scene."

Today, *A Hole in the Head* is chiefly remembered for introducing the song "High Hopes." Written by Sammy Cahn and Jimmy Van Heusen, who wrote numerous songs for Sinatra throughout his career, "High Hopes" won an Academy Award for Best Song and became a popular hit on the airwaves. As a testament to the cultural influence of Sinatra, it was even slightly reworked and used as a campaign song for John F. Kennedy during his 1960 presidential campaign.

"You expect me to change my way of life? Be you, instead of me? Not a chance. You can take your big brother sanctimonious act back to New York and turn blue."

Tony

NEVER SO FEW

AN MGM PICTURE | 1959

Director
John Sturges

Screenplay
Millard Kaufman

Based on the novel by Tom T. Chamales

Principal Cast
Frank Sinatra (Capt. Tom Reynolds), Gina Lollobrigida (Carla Vesari), Peter Lawford (Capt. Grey Travis), Steve McQueen (Bill Ringa), Richard Johnson (Capt. Danny De Mortimer), Paul Henreid (Nikko Regas), Brian Donlevy (Gen. Sloan), Dean Jones (Sgt. Jim Norby), Charles Bronson (Sgt. John Danforth)

FOURTEEN YEARS after the end of World War II Hollywood was still reluctant to make films that addressed the moral questions of war, but the public was already engaged in the debate. Frank Sinatra decided to fuel the discussion, and cinema was his medium of choice. He produced for MGM a film adaption of Tom T. Chamales novel *Never So Few*, a wartime romance in which the actions of soldiers in battle are questioned by their comrades even as they occur. Adding to the film's complexity is Sinatra's choice to play against type; he's a hero one moment, and an anti-hero the next, engaging in outrageous acts and leaving it to the other characters, and the audience, to be the judge.

Never So Few takes place at the start of the war, when American and British O.S.S. commanders were training a small group of Kachin warriors in Burma to repel the Japanese army. In a jungle compound, U.S. Captain Tom Reynolds (Frank Sinatra) and British Captain Danny De Mortimer (Richard Johnson) lead the operation, encouraging their soldiers to relax and enjoy themselves as best as they can between Japanese attacks, incidents so frequent they barely raise a pulse in the young GIs. The company badly needs a doctor, so captains Reynolds and De Mortimer fly to Calcutta to make their case to the army brass and engage in a few nights of revelry. During their first night on the town they meet the wealthy war

"You're on the green side of twenty-five, you're put together like a Christmas package, and you remind me of a pretty girl I once saw in a perfume ad before I became a lonely soldier."

Capt. Tom Reynolds (Sinatra) to Carla Vesari
(Gina Lollobrigida)

"You're off on a great adventure, living in the middle of a travel poster, and all because you found in yourself a rare ability—for violence."

Carla Vesari to Capt. Tom Reynolds

Left: Sinatra as Capt. Tom Reynolds.

Right: Reynolds is fascinated by Carla Vesari a bored socialite who considers him a rube.

profiteer Nikko Regas (Paul Henreid) and his mistress Carla Vesari (Gina Lollobrigida) and soon they're enjoying the hospitality of Regas' country estate, where Reynolds is doing his best to charm the cool and cutting Carla. She's annoyed by Reynolds at first, then enchanted, but the affair is rocky because the captain must soon return to the war. Heading back to the fighting, he brings the reluctant military doctor Capt. Grey Travis (Peter Lawford) and a soldier named Bill Ringa (Steve McQueen) who appeals to Reynolds because he's a maverick and a bootlegger, and quick with a jeep or any weapon that's tossed into his hands. The battle heats up, and Reynolds decides he's going to resolve the conflict by running his own little war, crossing into Chinese territory even at the risk of creating an international incident.

The casting for *Never So Few* is inspired, with the most important supporting player being Steve McQueen as Ringa. McQueen had established himself the previous year with the lead role in *The Blob* (1958) but he was playing a teenager at age twenty-eight, and his follow-up role in *The Great St. Louis Bank Robbery* (1959) was also a less-than-perfect fit.

Above: Rising star Steve McQueen (right) was chosen by Sinatra for the role of Bill Ringa.

Opposite: Far from the battle in Burma, Capt. Tom Reynolds and Capt. Danny De Mortimer (Richard Johnson) settle in for a night of heavy drinking.

But with *Never So Few* audiences got their first look at the screen persona that would soon make McQueen a marquee star—the cool antiauthoritarian, fast behind the wheel, and ready to roll with the punches. From his first moment onscreen in *Never So Few*, slumped behind the wheel of a parked jeep and chewing gum, the character's machismo is so clearly established one can't help but wonder how Ringa would have been played by Sinatra's first choice for the part: Sammy Davis, Jr. The diminutive crooner, a longtime Sinatra friend and protégé, was slated for the part until the two had a falling out based on remarks Davis made to a radio interviewer. Davis had been critical of Sinatra's behavior and, perhaps most damning, had told the interviewer that he considered himself the number one singer in America. The two patched up their differences soon after, but when filming for *Never So Few* began, Davis was out.

Sinatra made other excellent casting choices for *Never So Few*, assembling a large group of talented actors, including a few unknowns who would go on to stardom in the years to come. Charles Bronson, with many television appearances to his credit but no memorable film roles, was chosen to play the quick-fisted hothead Sgt. John Danforth, a character type that he would return to many times as he came into his own as a leading man. Dean Jones, a regular in 1960s Disney fare such as *The Love Bug* (1969) brings his boyish charm to the role of Sgt. Jim Norby, the bespectacled radio operator who reads comic books while machine guns rattle around him.

Sinatra also cast well-known stars in *Never So Few*, including Peter Lawford, soon to become part of the Sinatra film and stage ensemble known as the Rat Pack. Lawford adds the moral consciousness to the picture, with the worldly Dr. Trevis challenging Reynolds to justify violent acts he commits in the name of war. Gina Lollobrigida, an enormously popular sex symbol at the time, was included in the cast to create sexual tension with Sinatra's Capt. Reynolds, and to be featured in titillating situations, as when she invites Reynolds into her bathroom while she takes a bath. Lollobrigida's character is limited to two essential duties: to rebuff

Opposite top: Reynolds and De Mortimer enjoy the hospitality of Nikko Regas (Paul Henreid) at his country estate.

Opposite center: Ringa quickly bandages a wounded Reynolds after an attack on their compound.

Opposite bottom: Charles Bronson as Norby.

Reynolds for a few scenes, then to melt in his arms as he talks about domestic bliss and babies.

Never So Few takes the viewer from exciting battle scenes to champagne-and-chandelier parties, a balance of sub-plots that some reviewers found to be a cultural throwback despite the film's modern themes. "It looks as though Frank Sinatra has been tapped to succeed Errol Flynn," wrote Bosley Crowther in the *New York Times* after the film's premiere in December 1959. Philip K. Scheuer in the *Los Angeles Times* wrote that it "seems like an old-fashioned movie about an old-fashioned war," but added astutely, "it is almost sure to be popular."

With more than two dozen films to his credit before starring in *Never So Few*, Sinatra was a seasoned pro in Hollywood, but he hadn't become too jaded to learn something new. In the years that followed he would continue to place himself in leading roles, but he carried with him the lesson he learned from *Never So Few*: Surround yourself with a talented cast, then step back from time to time and give the newcomers their chance to shine.

Opposite: The aftermath of battle.

Below: Reynolds leads his men on a surprise attack.

Sinatra's cameo appearance in
Around the World in Eighty Days
(1956).

OTHER SINATRA FILMS

1953–1959

MEET ME IN LAS VEGAS
AN MGM PICTURE · 1956

DIRECTOR | Roy Rowland

SCREENPLAY | Isobel Lennart

PRINCIPAL CAST | Dan Dailey (Chuck Rodwell), Cyd Charisse (Maria Corvier), Agnes Moorehead (Miss Hattie), Jim Backus (Tom Culdane), Lili Darvas (Sari Hatvani)

Sinatra makes a cameo appearance in this minor MGM musical, a glitzy CinemaScope production about a rancher (Dailey) falling for a ballerina (Charisse), written by *The Kissing Bandit* screenwriter Isobel Lennart.

AROUND THE WORLD IN EIGHTY DAYS
A UNITED ARTISTS RELEASE · 1956

DIRECTOR | Michael Anderson

SCREENPLAY | James Poe, John Farrow, and S. J. Perelman
Based on the novel by Jules Verne

PRINCIPAL CAST | David Niven (Phineas Fogg), Cantinflas (Passepartout), Shirley MacLaine (Princess Aouda), Robert Newton (Inspector Fix), Noel Coward (Hesketh Baggott), Robert Morley (Ralph)

Producer Mike Todd recruited more than forty stars to play cameo roles in his epic, Academy Award–winning film version of the Jules Verne novel. Sinatra makes a wordless, blink-and–you-miss-him appearance as a piano player in a Barbary Coast saloon run by Marlene Dietrich.

The Sinatra of *Robin and the 7 Hoods*.

PART 3

THE RAT PACK YEARS

1960–1964

I F, as biographer Derek Jewell claimed, Sinatra enjoyed living out the fantasy of the Italian *padrone*—generous but ruthless, conducting business and personal affairs according to a credo of loyalty and faith—the Kennedy era would test that fantasy against the cold realities of both Hollywood and Washington, D.C. politics. By mid-decade, his political allegiance would shift from the Democratic to

the Republican Party and he would part ways with Capitol Records, a portion of his Las Vegas business holdings, and at least one romantic relationship.

The release of *Ocean's Eleven* in 1960 established the Rat Pack—Sinatra, Sammy Davis, Jr., Dean Martin, Joey Bishop, and Peter Lawford—as a force in Hollywood. Now the "Clan," as they were otherwise known, focused on becoming a political force. They campaigned throughout the election year on behalf of John F. Kennedy, Jr. Most of them, including Sinatra, had been lifelong Democrats, but more crucially, Lawford was the presidential candidate's

brother-in-law, having married Patricia Kennedy in 1954. In a show of supreme loyalty, Sinatra even ended a business partnership with blacklisted novelist Albert Maltz when it became political dynamite, threatening to harm JFK's campaign.

Sinatra, however, soon found his fealty repaid with continued rumors of his links to *Mafiosi*. And an investigation into his personal affairs, initiated by would-be Attorney General Robert Kennedy, only added insult to injury. Though the investigation yielded no conclusive evidence of mob dealings, Bobby Kennedy advised his brother to distance himself from Sinatra. The link was finally severed in 1962, when JFK turned down an invitation to visit Sinatra in Palm Springs, choosing instead to spend his time with Sinatra's longtime idol, Bing Crosby.

The following year, a battle with Bobby Kennedy appeared imminent after mobster Sam Giancana paid an unwelcome visit to Sinatra's Lake Tahoe Cal-Neva Casino. The incident might have been overlooked had the Nevada State Gaming Commission not banned Giancana from the gaming tables and had Kennedy not been intent on rooting out the racketeers. In a rare concession, Sinatra backed down from his initial support of Giancana, divesting himself from his casino holdings before the whole matter exploded out of control.

In the midst of all this turmoil, Sinatra gave one of his finest performances in John Frankenheimer's *The Manchurian Candidate* (1962). Though overlooked by the Motion Picture Academy, Sinatra's performance once again proved his talent and raw magnetism, and let him shine above the scandals. In 2005, *Time* magazine's Richard Corliss and Richard Schickel named *The Manchurian Candidate* one of the one hundred greatest films of all time.

Musically, too, Sinatra was ready to move on, and from 1961 to 1962, he fought Capitol Records over legal rights to his music as he established his own label, Reprise Records. The public battle worked in Sinatra's favor, sending sales of his Capitol releases soaring and boosting his Reprise albums to the top of the charts. He even outsold Elvis Presley, whom he had hosted in 1960's *Welcome Home, Elvis* television special. The generous royalties from the Capitol sales allowed him to pay off Reprise's debts,

and position the label as an artistic juggernaut. He explored various jazz influences, working with such heavyweights as Count Basie, Duke Ellington, and Bing Crosby. He turned fifty in 1965, and he began to show a fuller, more mature musical expression appropriate to his age and experience, setting him apart from youth culture and rock 'n' roll.

Sinatra's personal life, as usual, was not without its strife. In 1961, his engagement to dancer Juliet Prowse ended after an unimpressive six weeks; she had no interest in becoming the subservient wife Sinatra expected. In 1964, his only son, Frank, Jr., was kidnapped from his motel room near Harrah's Casino in Lake Tahoe. Sinatra worked with the FBI and paid a $240,000 ransom. The three kidnappers were caught shortly thereafter, leaving Sinatra to persuade the courts and the public that the whole thing had not been a publicity stunt.

That year, however, while working on *Von Ryan's Express*, he met a gamine who would later become his third wife: Mia Farrow. She was thirty years his junior, the daughter of actress Maureen O'Sullivan and, like Prowse, a "new woman" with an independent spirit. She was in love, however, and the press waited breathlessly to see where the romance would lead. Sinatra was poised to enter a quieter, more reflective phase in his life.

Sinatra on stage in top form.

CAN-CAN

A TWENTIETH CENTURY-FOX PICTURE | 1960

Director
Walter Lang

Screenplay
Dorothy Kingsley and Charles
Lederer
Based on the stage musical by
Abe Burrows and Cole Porter

Principal Cast
Frank Sinatra (Francois Durnais),
Shirley MacLaine (Simone
Pistache), Maurice Chevalier
(Paul Barriere), Louis Jourdan
(Philipe Forrestier), Juliet
Prowse (Claudine)

A MUSICAL CONFECTION about love, marriage and high kicks, *Can-Can* gives Sinatra the opportunity to croon some Cole Porter standards in his thirty-fourth feature film. Based on the Tony Award-winning 1953 Broadway hit, Walter Lang's film casts Sinatra in a breezy, affable role which he grants a certain necessary measure of gravitas.

Set in 1896 Montmartre, *Can-Can* centers around the café Bal du Paradis, where the "lewd and lascivious" can-can provides the illegal nightly entertainment. The café is run by Simone Pastiche (Shirley MacLaine), a savvy businesswoman who bribes most of the local gendarmes to look the other way. She has also forged an on-again/off-again affair with Francois Durnais (Sinatra), a womanizing lawyer who lends his legal services whenever Simone lands in hot water. Indeed, the café is raided at the film's outset, and Francois, along with the gentle judge, Paul Barriere (Maurice Chevalier), barely escape being arrested themselves.

When a formal complaint is filed against Simone, Francois defends her against a prudish judge, Philipe Forrestier (Jourdan), and eventually convinces him to drop the charges. But Forrestier isn't quite done with Simone just yet and attempts an entrapment scheme. Simone slips out of his grip, but much to his own surprise, Forrestier finds himself caught in hers—he falls in love. When he shocks her by proposing marriage, Simone

> **"Eliminate marriage and you'll never see any such thing as an unfaithful husband."**
>
> ·····
>
> Francois Durnais (Sinatra)

> **"You look like a broken umbrella."**
>
> ·····
>
> Francois Durnais to Simone (Shirley MacLaine)

> **"The Entertainment Event of the Year!"**
>
> ·····
>
> *Can-Can* tagline

Simone demonstrates her flexibility to Francois and Paul (Maurice Chevalier).

When Simone lands in jail, she relies on Francois to bail her out.

must choose between her love for Francois and her desire to become a "respectable" woman by "marrying up."

Though *Can-Can* appears to be the perfect marriage between Cole Porter standards and Sinatra's velvet crooning, the film's journey from stage to screen almost annulled the union before it was allowed to happen. The vivacious musical, which ran for two years on Broadway and starred Gwen Verdon, was a hit with audiences, but when Hollywood bought the rights to *Can-Can*, it also inherited its latent script problems. The property changed hands several times before landing at Fox, where the reliable Dorothy Kingsley was hired to transform the stage play into a viable screen story and create a role that would suit Sinatra. When she left, the remaining work was left to Charles Lederer. What emerged from the process was a story that ran over two hours and seemed short on music. Three more Cole Porter songs were added to round out the soundtrack: "Let's Do It (Let's Fall in Love)," "Just One of Those Things," and "You Do Something to Me."

With his pick of leading ladies, Sinatra chose Shirley MacLaine, who had starred with him in *Some Came Running* (1958). The filmmakers also attempted to cash in on the popularity of Maurice Chevalier and Louis Jourdan, who had starred together in 1958's *Gigi*, to give *Can-Can* some authentic French flavor. Newcomer Juliet Prowse, who was then reportedly dating Sinatra, was given her first screen role and received praise even from the cantankerous Bosley Crowther of the *New York Times*.

Both critical and popular reaction to the film has remained mixed since its initial release. Although some reviewers write it off as flat, overlong, and clunky, others embrace the film and its musical numbers as a Technicolor celebration of fun. Released in 1960 but set in fin-de-siècle France, the story does send "mixed messages" about the shifting morality and social mores it's meant to critique. Old attitudes about sexuality and marriage receive an airing out and an occasionally witty examination. The story wants to be a loosening of the cultural corset, as it were, and celebrate a greater acceptance of sexuality. The plot, however, seems to work in retrograde, forcing its characters into more traditional mindsets.

Top: Francois and Paul woo the ladies of Montmartre.

Center: Sinatra with Juliet Prowse. She was his fiancée for six weeks.

Bottom: Sinatra and MacLaine perform a Cole Porter classic, "Let's Do It (Let's Fall in Love)."

Simone is a dance-hall hoofer and proprietor who just wants to get married and settle down. Francois, who would just as soon outlaw marriage, is forced to settle down and make the café owner an honest woman if he wants to keep her. Perhaps the studio wasn't entirely ready to kick up its moral heels—or perhaps Nikita Khrushchev's now legendary visit to the set and alleged outrage at its moral lassitude forced a more conservative approach.

More than one reviewer, including Crowther, has noted, too, that the direction by Walter Lang, whom the studio itself referred to as a "journeyman," seems stiff and wooden. The camera remains static throughout much of the dance numbers, and the actors never seem completely at home. Choreographer Hermes Pan, Fred Astaire's longtime collaborator, compensates, however, with visually striking dance numbers. The standouts, for audiences and reviewers alike, are MacLaine's "Apache Dance" and the "Adam and Eve" number featuring MacLaine and Prowse.

Most fittingly, though, Sinatra himself gets one of the film's better moments, crooning "It's All Right With Me" to would-be love interest Claudine (Prowse). He casually invites the audience into the moment as he tries to let the poor girl down easy. The song's subtext is rich with feeling, and Sinatra's performance is pitch-perfect. It's one of the first times we're made to understand just how deep his feelings run. It's also a keen reminder of the romantic leading man Sinatra was capable of being, given the opportunity and the room to do it.

Though *Can-Can* may not hold up to musicals such as *Pal Joey*, more and more it seems contemporary audiences are not ready to dismiss it, and perhaps they're right not to. For all its shortcomings, it maintains a *joie de vivre*, a winking sense that perhaps, in the right circumstances, social mores can change like fashion. Its wit still rings true, and then there is the music of Cole Porter. As Jourdan observes, "It's so hard to quarrel with a melody." If Sinatra's singing it, the argument is already won.

Opposite top: Choreographer Hermes Pan, best known for his collaborations with Fred Astaire, staged a visceral and demanding dance number for Shirley MacLaine.

Opposite bottom: Best known for his role in *Gigi* (1958), Louis Jourdan co-starred as Philippe, a stuffy judge enforcing the local morality laws. Here Paul offers musical advice to Philippe with "Just One of Those Things."

Above: At a low point, Francois
looks for a little diversion.

Opposite: The film's elaborate
"Adam and Eve" dance sequence.
Can-Can received two Academy
Award nominations, for Best
Costume Design and Best Original
Music Score.

OCEAN'S ELEVEN

A WARNER BROS. PICTURE | 1960

Director

Lewis Milestone

Screenplay

Harry Brown and Charles Lederer

Principal Cast

Frank Sinatra (Danny Ocean),
Dean Martin (Sam Harmon),
Sammy Davis, Jr. (Josh Howard),
Peter Lawford (Jimmy Foster),
Joey Bishop ("Mushy"
O'Connors), Angie Dickinson
(Beatrice Ocean), Richard Conte
(Tony Bergdorf), Cesar Romero
(Duke Santos), Buddy Lester
(Vince Massler), Akim Tamiroff
(Spyros Acebos)

IN 1960, the life Frank Sinatra was living was a source of public fascination, fueled by a media anxious to celebrate, label, promote, and exaggerate what appeared to be a new brand of hedonism for the New Frontier. Ensconced in the Sands hotel and casino in Las Vegas, Sinatra had surrounded himself with his closest friends in the entertainment business and was leading the group in an almost nonstop work-and-play lifestyle of his own invention: Party and perform on stage every night at the Sands, continue the party off-stage until the wee hours, catch a few hours sleep, and roll onto the set sometime after noon to film scenes for a motion picture, *Ocean's Eleven.*

In *Ocean's Eleven* Sinatra plays Danny Ocean, a former World War II sergeant who decides to reunite his unit in Las Vegas to pull a major heist: the robbery of five casinos simultaneously on New Year's Eve. The ten men he assembles have followed Ocean into battle and they won't desert him now, especially since the crime itself is certain to give them that old feeling again—the spark of excitement they felt together in the war, and subsequently lost at war's end. Central to the crew are Jimmy Foster (Peter Lawford), a wealthy mama's boy with nothing but free time; Sam Harmon (Dean Martin) a gadfly and lounge singer; "Mushy" O'Connors (Joey Bishop), a former boxer; and Josh Howard (Sammy Davis, Jr.), a baseball

> ## "Frank! Dean! Sammy! Peter! Angie! Who else could make such terrific excitement and have such fun doing it!"
>
> ....
>
> **Advertisement for *Ocean's Eleven***

His team assembled, Danny Ocean spells out his plan to rob five Las Vegas casinos simultaneously.

> ## "Why waste all those cute little tricks that the army taught us just because it's sort of peaceful now?"
>
> ....
>
> **Danny Ocean (Sinatra) to Vince Massler (Buddy Lester) and Jimmy Foster (Peter Lawford)**

Top: While waiting for the rest of the eleven to arrive, Sam Harmon (Dean Martin) and Jimmy Foster (Peter Lawford) enjoy cocktails in the gang's comfortable hideaway.

Center: Danny Ocean passes the time in his hotel suite with a female companion.

Bottom: Josh Howard (Sammy Davis, Jr.) sings for his fellow garbage truck drivers.

player-turned-garbage man. The large ensemble cast also features Akim Tamiroff as the mastermind Spyros Acebos, Buddy Lester as Ocean's recruiter Vince Massler, Cesar Romero as a local highroller, and Angie Dickinson as Ocean's estranged wife Beatrice.

Written by Harry Brown and Charles Lederer, *Ocean's Eleven* takes its time introducing the characters as they leisurely arrive one by one, but once the gang is together and Ocean explains the plan, the action starts to move. They case each casino, working out a few logistics, and quickly the heist is underway, with a different team of robbers positioned at each location. The suspense builds from the fact that Ocean's team has no guns and no criminal experience, and little idea what it is they're doing. Up until that point in the film, the collective skill of the gang seems to be only in enjoying themselves and approaching every aspect of the high life with an abundance of cool.

The premise and story add only slightly to the film's overall appeal. The attraction of *Ocean's Eleven* is the glimpse it gives of the highly publicized real-life camaraderie and hijinks of its stars and those who orbited them—a show biz microcosm touted in *Playboy* magazine as "the innest in-group in the world." For a series of dates at the Sands, Sinatra was joined by Martin, Bishop, Lawford and Davis, and the entire country was buzzing about what the group, dubbed "The Rat Pack," was doing on stage. Their twice-nightly shows were the hottest ticket in town, with thousands of tourists turned away while people of influence, including Senator John F. Kennedy, settled in to watch Sinatra and friends joke and sing together on stage. A bar cart was wheeled out so the performers could drink, or pretend to, as they worked through the act, and the atmosphere of carefree debauchery amazed audiences night after night. They made racial and ethnic jokes about themselves and each other, referred to woman as "broads," and wandered around the stage smoking and drinking and creating the impression that only their level of inebriation would determine where the show would go next. Audiences couldn't get enough of the spectacle. Sinatra knew it would work on film as well.

> **"The way I figure it is like this: The eleven of us cats against this one little city? We're in overlay."**
>
> Josh Howard (Sammy Davis, Jr.) to Vince Massler

Above: Josh, Sam, Danny, and Jimmy debate how best to spend their millions.

Opposite: The Las Vegas of the Rat Pack era.

Ocean's Eleven captures a portion of the Rat Pack's public image, the vision of middle-aged men lounging in hotel suites, a drink always within easy reach, while female companions drift around the edges of the scene or find themselves summarily dismissed. Light humor floats among the men, much of it ad-libbed during filming, but never to the point of laughter; the coolness of the characters, after all, derives from the fact that they seem to be always saving their energy for the real party, still to come.

The musical aspects of the Rat Pack stage show, however, are mostly absent from *Ocean's Eleven*. Sinatra doesn't sing at all while Davis and Martin perform one song each. But the film blurs the lines between the film's characters and the entertainers who play them, as when they kid with Lawford, who was Kennedy's brother-in-law, about using his family fortune to buy a political office. In one shot, the characters saunter along the Las Vegas Strip, passing a Sands marquee that bears their real names, a nod to the legend they had created, and to the real show they'd be performing later that night.

Film critics noted the movie's casual style and pacing, but highlighting that fact only assured moviegoers that *Ocean's Eleven* was just the type of entertainment they hoped it would be. "It is all so genial," a review in *Newsweek* asserted, "that the major suspense lies in whether Frank, Dean, et al., will get their hands out of their pockets long enough to pull the robbery which the movie is all about." *Variety* noted that the film "never quite makes its point, but romps along merrily unconcerned that it doesn't." Armed with this knowledge, audiences flocked to see *Ocean's Eleven* in the summer of 1960 and placed it among the top ten highest-grossing films of the year.

Sinatra enjoyed working on *Ocean's Eleven*, and relaxed into his role with the assurance that, though they weren't creating high art, they were making a film that was sure to entertain and make a profit. Though he couldn't have known it at the time, *Ocean's Eleven* also proved to be a milestone in Sinatra's movie career. It's a film still celebrated today, not just for its attitude and ambiance, but for the tantalizing glimpse it seemingly offers viewers of Sinatra's off-screen life.

"There's only one thing you love, Danny. That's danger."

Beatrice Ocean (Angie Dickinson) to Danny Ocean

Top: The deal is sealed.

Center: Danny makes a fleeting attempt to reconcile with his estranged wife Beatrice.

Bottom: As payment for her uncredited appearance in *Ocean's Eleven*, Shirley MacLaine (with Martin) received a new car.

Above: Danny scopes out the scene in preparation for the heist.

Right: With other *Ocean's Eleven* cast members, the legendary Rat Pack strolls in front of the Sands.

THE DEVIL AT 4 O'CLOCK

AN MGM RELEASE | 1961

Director

Mervyn LeRoy

Screenplay

Liam O'Brien

Based on the novel by Max Catto

Principal Cast

Spencer Tracy (Father Doonan),
Frank Sinatra (Harry),
Grégoire Aslan (Marcel), Bernie
Hamilton (Charlie), Kerwin
Mathews (Father Perreau), Jean-
Pierre Aumont (Jacques),
Barbara Luna (Camille), Martin
Brandt (Doctor Wexler),
Alexander Scourby (the
governor)

WITH A $5 MILLION BUDGET—$1 million less than *The Guns of Navarone* (1961) and $2 million more than *The Bridge on the River Kwai* (1957)—this high-concept, high-adventure, first-time pairing of Spencer Tracy and Frank Sinatra represented a sizable investment for MGM. Veteran director Mervyn LeRoy, who had scored a hit for the studio with the epic *Quo Vadis* (1951), was hired to guide two of Hollywood's biggest stars in this adaptation of Max Catto's novel, which unfolds against the backdrop of an imminent volcanic eruption in the South Pacific.

Sinatra had always wanted to work with Tracy, and the respect was mutual. Though Tracy's character drives the action of this film, he generously said, "Nobody has his power. *The Devil at 4 O'Clock* was a Sinatra picture. Sinatra was the star." And Sinatra certainly comes off as a likeable character—for a criminal. *The Devil at 4 O'Clock* is in the tradition of bad men turning good that made *3 Godfathers* (1948) and *We're No Angels* (1955) so popular. Is there a bigger arc for characters to travel than from corrupt and uncaring to suddenly saintly? As the story gets underway, writer Liam O'Brien and director Mervyn Le Roy waste no time blurring the line between good and evil.

Sinatra plays Harry, who with his equally dangerous and self-centered convict friends, Marcel (Grégoire Aslan) and Charlie (Bernie

"A small volcanic South Seas
isle makes a colorful setting for
this tale of heroism and sacrifice,
but vying with interest in
characterizations are the
exceptional special effects of an
island being blown to pieces."

Variety

Left: Harry puts the moves on Camille (Barbara Luna), a beautiful blind girl.

Right: Father Doonan (Spencer Tracy) and Harry (Sinatra) lock horns. Sinatra had so much respect for Tracy that he agreed to take second billing.

"It's hard for a man to be brave
when he knows he is going to meet
the devil at 4 o'clock."

Epigraph from *The Devil at 4 O'Clock* (Spanish proverb)

Top: Sinatra and Barbara Luna.

Center: Father Doonan rescues Harry from the island prison "hold."

Bottom: The volcano is an imposing, smoldering presence in Mervyn LeRoy's big-budget disaster film.

Hamilton), is being transported to a prison in Tahiti, where they'll serve eight years. We never learn what they did to earn that sentence, only that someone was killed during their last jailbreak. When the plane transporting the criminals stops overnight in Talua, where they're dropping off a new priest and picking up the old one, we're introduced to a fairly unsaintly Father Doonan (Tracy), a priest for whom parishioners have an obvious disdain.

The good father drinks just after waking, and it's plain to see that he has more cynicism than faith. That's the first thing his replacement, Father Perreau (Kerwin Matthews), notices. The second is the liquor bottle prominently displayed. But all is not what it seems. Father Perreau soon learns the reason Father Doonan drinks and why he's lost his faith. He wanted to build a hospital for leprous children in the islands, and the locals fought him. They were afraid it would hurt tourism. Though he built his hospital high in the mountains far away from town, the islanders never went to one of Father Doonan's masses again. He's forced to grab what he can, and that means pouncing when new convicts come to the island. As Father Doonan

> **"In the great high-adventure tradition of *The Guns of Navarone* and *The Bridge On The River Kwai*!"**
>
> *The Devil at 4 O'Clock* tagline

The Devil at 4 O'Clock features special effects by Willis Cook, who later worked on the pilot for the television series *Bewitched*.

informs the governor (Alexander Scourby), he's entitled to convict labor, so he drives into the compound, removes the three convicts from an underground "hold," and puts them to work repairing his hospital.

Viewers are expected to forgive Father Doonan for his alcoholism, his ruthlessness, his pugnacious attitude, and his obvious lack of faith—small things compared to the larger good that he's accomplishing. That, of course, invites a moralistic comparison with the convicts. Are they really as bad as they seem? When the volcano threatens the village and people must evacuate, it's Harry who convinces his convict buddies to volunteer to be air-dropped over the hospital to help Father Doonan try to rescue the children and staff. Are the convicts motivated by the priest's promise to put in a good word for them, or is it the speech he gave the townspeople: "If you turn away now, all your lives you'll torture yourself with the awful memory of what you have done." Or, in Harry's case, is it self-interest? He's fallen for a blind girl, Camille (Barbara Luna), who's spent most of her life at Father Doonan's hospital. Is Harry preying on the woman, or treating her like any woman without her handicap would want to be treated? Is he returning just to save her, or does he really care about the children, or helping the priest? The more we see, the more we realize that the characters in this film are more complex than typical disaster-movie structure. The priest and children have an effect on the convicts, and the convicts have an effect on them.

Tracy turns in a powerful performance, and Sinatra is equally fine. It's the writing that produces unbelievably quick turnarounds, whether it's a governor giving permission to take convicts or Harry's remarkably quick-moving relationship with Camille. Director LeRoy also employs some pretty heavy-handed foreshadowing, as when a camera continues to focus on a patch of earth that looks loose as a trap door about to give way, and, sure enough, it finally does. But the special effects are quite good, and the acting is solid enough to compensate for moments of melodrama and logical inconsistencies.

Filmed in and around Lahaina, Hawaii, *The Devil at 4 O'Clock* was one of the most elaborate films Sinatra ever made. It took a half-million

Top: Harry quickly takes on a leadership role.

Center: Disaster strikes.

Bottom: Harry and the others carry the smallest and weakest children as they try to escape the lava flow.

dollars just to build the town and put thirty-six special effects experts to work rigging it to break apart as if it were the result of a real earthquake and volcanic eruption. As for the crater, it was constructed in flat California farmland but ended up looking so real that it would be used for stock footage of volcanic eruptions by future filmmakers.

Despite the buzz surrounding the teaming of Sinatra and Tracy, the film was only a modest success and received favorable, if underwhelming critical notices. *Variety* called Sinatra's performance "first class but minor" compared to Tracy's, but then again, even Tracy has to compete with a volcano for the audience's attention.

During the filming of *The Devil at 4 O'Clock*, a *New York Times* reporter visited the set and wrote this evocative description of the star: "Sinatra, lolling in a canvas chair under a real palm tree, admitted that he would go on hacking his way through the rough terrain of show business as long as his legs and acting ability held out." Truth be told, Sinatra didn't spend much time "lolling in a canvas chair" while in Hawaii. The 1960 presidential election was months away. When he wasn't required to be on the set, he used his downtime to barnstorm the islands in a private plane, stumping for his good friend John F. Kennedy.

SERGEANTS 3

A UNITED ARTISTS RELEASE | 1962

Director
John Sturges

Screenplay
W. R. Burnett

Principal Cast
Frank Sinatra (1st Sgt. Mike Merry), Dean Martin (Sgt. Chip Deal), Sammy Davis, Jr. (Jonah Williams), Peter Lawford (Sgt. Larry Barrett), Joey Bishop (Sgt.-Maj. Roger Boswell), Henry Silva (Mountain Hawk), Ruta Lee (Amelia)

FRANK SINATRA had so much fun making the 1960 caper comedy *Ocean's Eleven* with his cadre of famous friends that he decided to do it again. In fact, he envisioned five "Rat Pack" films in five years. It did not quite work out that way, but *Sergeants 3* (1962) came close to replicating the experience of *Ocean's Eleven*, even as the milieu changed from the buddies' comfort zone of smoky, contemporary Las Vegas casinos to the canyons and mesas of the nineteenth-century Southwest. That party atmosphere worked its way onscreen, as an action western that begins with the massacre of an entire town evolves into a broad comedy tailored to its stars' personalities.

After the Wanagi Wacipi, or Ghost Dancers, a renegade Native American tribe, murder the inhabitants of Medicine Bend, 1st Sgt. Mike Merry (Sinatra), Sgt. Chip Deal (Dean Martin), and Sgt. Larry Barrett (Peter Lawford) are sent to investigate and later garrison the remote outpost. Aware that they are already in trouble with their commanding officer for their part in a saloon brawl, Merry insists on following orders not to pursue the Ghost Dancers. That is fine with Barrett, who is about to leave the service and marry his fiancée Amelia (Ruta Lee). But egged on by ex-slave Jonah Williams (Sammy Davis, Jr.), who hopes that a demonstration of his own bravery will earn him a spot in the army, Deal seeks the glory of battle—and is determined to drag his friends along with him.

"You men are sworn to protect the property of the people of this community. Not break it up or smash it up. Is that clear?"

Col. William Collingwood (Richard Simmons), chastizing
1st Sgt. Mike Merry (Sinatra), Sgt. Chip Deal (Dean Martin), and
Sgt. Larry Barrett (Peter Lawford)

First Sgt. Mike Merry, Sgt. Chip Deal, and Sgt. Larry Barrett confront an angry buffalo hunter at the saloon.

"You know what I'm going to do? I'm going to make a hero out of you, a hero out of me, and a hero out of good old Larry."

Deal warning Merry of trouble brewing

Top: Merry recovering from a brawl with rampaging buffalo hunters.

Center: Freed slave Jonah (Sammy Davis, Jr.) makes the acquaintance of the title characters.

Bottom: Ghost Dancer Mountain Hawk (Henry Silva) surprises Merry and Willie Sharpknife (Buddy Lester) when they investigate the mysterious goings on in Medicine Bend.

Helmed by John Sturges and written by veteran novelist and screenwriter W. R. Burnett, this loose riff on Rudyard Kipling's *Gunga Din* reflects the schizophrenic divide between serious moviemakers and fun-seeking stars. The action scenes, particularly the opening massacre and an initial skirmish between the cavalry and the Ghost Dancers, are superbly staged. The movie is also gorgeous, thanks to exterior locations in Utah's Bryce National Park and sublime widescreen camerawork by Best Cinematography Oscar-winner Winton C. Hoch, a frequent John Ford collaborator. Less successful are the performances, which more accurately can be described as mugging rather than acting. The broad, winking humor might have worked better if Burnett had more successfully integrated it into the story. Instead, too many comic bits are extraneous and tend to stop the movie cold. A subplot involving Merry and Deal's campaign to keep their friend Barrett not just in the army but also single is a bizarre bit of misogynistic "bromance" that generates few laughs.

Sinatra was intent on reviving the conviviality that marked the *Ocean's Eleven* set, going so far as to take money out of the film's budget to install connecting doors at the production's Kanab, Utah hotel to facilitate the party atmosphere. The fun went on even when they returned to Hollywood to shoot interiors. Frank Sinatra, Jr. remembered distaff Rat Pack member Shirley MacLaine, taking a break from filming *The Children's Hour* (1961) on the soundstage next door, walking through the set mid-take, her cheeks ballooned as if she had the mumps, calling out, "I'm eating chestnuts. Anybody want some?" The easily bored Sinatra was still antsy, particularly on the forty-minute helicopter flight that he and Martin made between Las Vegas, where they were performing at the Sands, and Kanab. One day, Martin whipped out a pair of .22 pistols midflight and the two entertained themselves firing out at the desert until Sinatra complained that Martin's shots were whizzing awfully close to his face. "Hell, I don't want you to be bored, right?" said Martin. "Coo-coo," replied Sinatra as he resumed shooting.

The shenanigans did not amuse everyone. Actor Tony Curtis, on a photo assignment from *Ebony* magazine, was frustrated as they turned his

Above: Merry and Deal resort to hand-to-hand combat with the Ghost Dancers in a bid to stop their escape.

Opposite: Answering director John Sturges' challenge, Sinatra performed his own stunts in a scene where Merry is first dragged by a buckboard and then clings to it as he works his way back to the top.

The Calvary tries to stop the Ghost
Dancers reign of terror in an all-out
battle.

attempt at photography into a comedy routine. "Until I could melt into the scenery and they forgot about me, I could only go through the motions," he recalled. Sturges succeeded in getting Sinatra to take at least one of the action sequences more seriously when he challenged him to perform his own stunt in a scene where Merry struggles beneath a buckboard while Deal battles Indians on top. "I didn't mind the dragging, but what really bothered me was the way Dean kept stomping on my fingers as he was thrown back and forth," Sinatra later recalled.

Rat Pack Confidential author Shawn Levy theorizes that when it comes to Rat Pack movie titles—*Ocean's Eleven, Sergeants 3, Four for Texas,* and *Robin and the 7 Hoods*—"real meaning lay in the number itself. . . . 11, 3, 4, and 7: Frank was shooting craps with house money." As far as *Sergeants 3*'s critics were concerned, this time Sinatra crapped out. "Mr. Sinatra and his loyal coterie switch from slapstick to slaughter and back again with reckless abandon. They may have found a 'home' in this peculiar kind of an 'Army' but their antics may be enough to give a discerning observer the megrims," sniffed the *New York Times'* A. H. Weiler. *Time* magazine was even more contemptuous, writing, "The Clansmen loaf kiddingly through their parts, acquiring suntans . . . Perceptive viewers will realize that Sinatra and his Cub Scout troupe are pioneering in a new art form: the $4,000,000 home movie." "It is more din than *Gunga Din,* starting with a barroom brawl and ending with a howling massacre," complained Hazel Flynn in the *Hollywood Citizen-News.*

Audiences were more forgiving, as *Sergeants 3* went on to moderate success, earning $4.3 million at the box office. But perhaps the fans sensed that the party might be winding down. For though there would be two more "Rat Pack" movies and the stars would continue to work in various combinations together through the years, *Sergeants 3* marked the last time that all of them—Sinatra, Martin, Davis, Lawford, and Bishop—would share the screen together. Regardless of the quality of *Sergeants 3,* the western motif seems appropriate as the Rat Pack rode off into the sunset.

"I know you've been in touch with the Duke, with John Wayne. I know that you have been studying how to be in a Western picture. Therefore, I'm going to give you a test to see how well you might or might not have done your homework."

Director John Sturges challenging Sinatra to perform a difficult stunt

THE MANCHURIAN CANDIDATE

A UNITED ARTISTS RELEASE | 1962

Director
John Frankenheimer

Screenplay
George Axelrod

Based on the novel by Richard
Condon

Principal Cast
Frank Sinatra (Bennett Marco),
Laurence Harvey (Raymond
Shaw), Janet Leigh (Rosie),
Angela Lansbury (Mrs. Iselin),
Henry Silva (Chunjin), James
Gregory (Senator John
Yerkes Iselin), Leslie Parrish
(Jocelyn Jordan), John McGiver
(Senator Thomas Jordan), Khigh
Dhiegh (Yen Lo)

UNITED ARTISTS PRESIDENT Arthur Krim was never one to shy away from controversy. In 1955, he had done the unthinkable and released Sinatra's *The Man with the Golden Arm* without the all-important Production Code's seal of approval. And he'd consistently green-lit risky fare like Charles Laughton's dreamlike thriller *The Night of the Hunter* (1955) and Stanley Kubrick's anti-war drama, *Paths of Glory* (1957). But *The Manchurian Candidate* made Krim nervous, for John Frankenheimer's proposed film version of Richard Condon's 1959 best-selling political thriller would depict a brainwashed Korean War veteran's mission to assassinate a presidential candidate. At a time when Cold War-era tensions were escalating between the United States and the Soviet Union, *The Manchurian Candidate*'s surreal mixture of conspiracy thriller and mordant black comedy struck Krim, then finance chairman of the Democratic Party, as both "un-American" and potentially offensive to JFK.

Sinatra, however, felt otherwise. When Frankenheimer and screenwriter George Axelrod (*The Seven Year Itch*) approached him to star in *The Manchurian Candidate*, Sinatra agreed without hesitation. As for Krim's concerns about offending JFK, Sinatra knew just how to assuage his worries. He'd simply have his good buddy in the Oval Office call Krim and give him the presidential thumbs up. In fact, JFK was a fan of

> "If you come in five minutes after this picture begins, you won't know what it's all about! When you've seen it all, you'll swear there's never been anything like it!"

The Manchurian Candidate tagline

> "It isn't as if Raymond's hard to like. He's impossible to like! In fact, he's probably one of the most repulsive human beings I've ever known."

Bennett Marco (Sinatra) on fellow soldier Raymond Shaw (Laurence Harvey)

Left: A jittery Korean War veteran Bennett Marco (Sinatra) struggles to maintain his composure under the watchful eye of Colonel Milt (Douglas Henderson).

Right: Sinatra gives one of his all-time greatest performances in John Frankenheimer's masterpiece, which inexplicably failed to receive a Best Picture Academy Award nomination.

Condon's novel and only had one question for Sinatra: "Who's playing the mother?"

The role of the mother, a power-mad, red-baiting senator's wife whose ambition is eclipsed only by her cold-blooded ruthlessness, seemed like a natural fit for either Bette Davis or Barbara Stanwyck. Yet Sinatra had a very different type of actress in mind for the juicy part: Lucille Ball. Although Ball had previously played an unsympathetic character to great effect in *The Big Street* (1942), she was now too closely identified with *I Love Lucy* for audiences to see her as the Beltway version of Lady Macbeth. Not that Frankenheimer actually said this to his famously combative star. He instead screened his film *All Fall Down* (1961) featuring Angela Lansbury as Warren Beatty's ultra-possessive mother, for Sinatra. Lansbury's hard-edged performance in the overheated family melodrama impressed Sinatra, and the thirty-seven-year-old British actress was cast as thirty-four-year-old Laurence Harvey's mother in *The Manchurian Candidate*.

With Janet Leigh rounding out the film's principal cast as Sinatra's love interest, Frankenheimer shot *The Manchurian Candidate* in forty-one days flat. Playing the troubled hero, an army captain plagued by nightmares of brainwashing and torture at the hands of Soviet and Chinese agents, Sinatra threw himself into the role. During a martial arts fight sequence—one of the first of its kind in American cinema—Sinatra broke a finger

Above: Beware the red queen: an arresting image from the opening credits.

Right: Marco catches the eye of Rosie (Janet Leigh).

Opposite top: The soldiers undergo brainwashing in one of the film's most surreal sequences.

Opposite bottom: The puppet master at work: Mrs. Iselin (Angela Lansbury) wields her power behind the scenes, controlling her husband, Senator Iselin (James Gregory, on screen).

Although just three older than Harvey, Lansbury convincingly portrays his mother in *The Manchurian Candidate*.

when he smashed his hand through an actual coffee table, rather than a breakaway prop.

Whatever pain Sinatra experienced was the proverbial small price to pay for the starring role in this brilliantly original and provocative film. It had been years since Sinatra had taken on such an emotionally and physically demanding role, one that required him to stretch beyond his image as the personification of cool. As Captain Bennett Marco, Sinatra gives a riveting, tightly wound performance that never descends into histrionics. There's little trace of the cocky Sinatra persona in the sweaty, psychologically frail Marco, who gradually unravels the sinister plot that's turned his former army comrade Raymond Shaw (Harvey) into a deadly "sleeper" assassin.

Save for a mixed review from *New York Times* critic Bosley Crowther, *The Manchurian Candidate* received mostly glowing notices from critics when United Artists released it in late October of 1962. Pauline Kael, the idiosyncratic queen bee of film critics, was positively effusive in her praise of *The Manchurian Candidate*: "This picture plays some wonderful, crazy games about the Right and the Left; although it's a thriller, it may be the most sophisticated political satire ever made in Hollywood."

Yet rave reviews and solid box office returns did not endear *The Manchurian Candidate* to the notoriously fickle Motion Picture Academy voters. When the 1962 Academy Award nominations were announced, *The Manchurian Candidate* was conspicuously missing from the Best Picture, Actor, and Director categories, among others. The film received only two nominations, for Best Editing and Best Supporting Actress (Lansbury), and lost both. Although Lansbury was considered a shoo-in for her Machiavellian turn, the Motion Picture Academy instead went the sentimental route and gave the Best Supporting Actress statuette to sixteen-year-old Patty Duke for playing Helen Keller in *The Miracle Worker* (1962).

Of course, *The Manchurian Candidate's* Oscar snub was quickly forgotten in the wake of JFK's assassination on November 22, 1963. Almost immediately, rumors sprang up that Sinatra had withdrawn the film from

> **"It's important to know that Frank Sinatra was a man who really was better on the first take. It wasn't a question of the fact that he would only do one take, as rumor has it sometimes. He was just better on the first take."**
>
> *The Manchurian Candidate*
> director John Frankenheimer

Top: A tense reunion between Marco and Laurence Harvey as Raymond Shaw, the unwitting assassin.

Center: Marco with Jocie (Leslie Parrish), Raymond's trusting bride.

Bottom: Alligators display more of a maternal instinct than Mrs. Iselin, who uses her son as a pawn in her sinister plan.

distribution in the wake of the national tragedy. Another whopper dreamed up by rabid conspiracy theorists hypothesized that JFK's alleged assassin Lee Harvey Oswald had studied *The Manchurian Candidate* as a blueprint. Over time, these groundless rumors gave rise to the urban legend that *The Manchurian Candidate* was a "lost" film, when nothing could have been further from the truth (although it was banned from Soviet bloc countries until the 1990s). It aired several times on network television throughout the 1960s and 1970s prior to its theatrical re-release in 1988. And contrary to rumor, Sinatra did not pull the film from distribution due to political concerns; the film's absence from the big screen was the result of a prolonged contractual dispute between Sinatra and United Artists.

Today, nearly fifty years after its premiere and a respectful 2004 remake that Sinatra himself had earlier suggested, *The Manchurian Candidate* is universally regarded as a masterpiece. Time has not diminished the film's startling power and political relevance. Of all Sinatra's films, *The Manchurian Candidate* is undeniably his best.

"Sinatra, in his usual uncanny fashion, is simply terrific."

New Yorker

Marco makes a last-ditch effort to de-program Raymond.

COME BLOW YOUR HORN

A PARAMOUNT PICTURE | 1963

Director
Bud Yorkin

Screenplay
Norman Lear

Based on the play by Neil Simon

Principal Cast
Frank Sinatra (Alan Baker),
Tony Bill (Buddy Baker), Lee J.
Cobb (Harry R. Baker), Molly
Picon (Sophie Baker), Barbara
Rush (Connie), Jill St. John
(Peggy John), Phyllis McGuire
(Mrs. Eckman)

FRANK SINATRA'S well-honed public image as the ultimate playboy naturally drew him to parts that celebrated the swinger lifestyle, but with *Come Blow Your Horn*, he opted for a change-up—a chance to walk the line between ultra-cool and ordinary. Sinatra was in good hands, with a story created by Neil Simon, a screenplay by Norman Lear, and direction by Bud Yorkin, a group that would go on to shape the face of American theater, film, and television for decades to come. It was a creative team that had already proven they were clever enough to work with comedy legends, but *Come Blow Your Horn* was their chance to show they were hip enough for Sinatra as well.

As the lead in *Come Blow Your Horn*, Sinatra provides every bit of cool the film has to offer. He plays Alan Baker, an employee at his father's artificial fruit business who never actually shows up for work, devoting his time instead to the über-bachelor lifestyle in his vast, modern apartment. As one female companion leaves Alan's pad and another arrives moments later, he shuffles his lies and excuses with all the calm and practice of a busy maitre d'. Into his blissful world comes younger brother Buddy (Tony Bill), who has finally left the nest at age twenty-one and arrived on Alan's doorstep ready to experience life, or at least a life that doesn't include his protective parents, Sophie (Molly Picon) and Harry (Lee J. Cobb). Alan

> "You've got looks and personality, and today that's all you need in the music business. Even the hockey players are making albums."
>
> ....
>
> Alan Baker (Sinatra) to Connie (Barbara Rush)

> "Twenty-one years old, already you're a bigger bum than your brother is and you got eighteen years to go."
>
> ....
>
> Harry Baker (Lee J. Cobb) to Buddy Baker (Tony Bill)

Left: The uber-bachelor in his element: from left to right, Barbara Rush, Phyllis McGuire, and Jill St. John with Sinatra.

Right: A Baker family portrait: Alan and his kid brother Buddy (Tony Bill) behind their ultra-protective parents Sophie (Molly Picon) and Harry (Lee J. Cobb).

happily introduces Buddy to martinis, then fixes him up with his sensuous but dim-witted neighbor, Peggy (Jill St. John), and educates his young protégé on the finer points of dating three women at once. But as Buddy slides into the swinger lifestyle, and a parade of parents and girlfriends march through the door, Alan decides it's time to find the calm at the center of this storm. Suddenly he realizes that one of his regular dates, Connie (Barbara Rush), is actually the love of his life.

Come Blow Your Horn is formulaic, but it was produced by the team who honed and refined the formula into a staple of American entertainment that endures to this day. Simon had started his career writing sketches for the brilliant 1950s television programs *Your Show of Shows* and *Caesar's Hour*, working alongside Mel Brooks, Woody Allen, and other young writers who would soon emerge as comedy stars. Simon's stage play *Come Blow Your Horn*, which opened on Broadway in 1961 and became a hit, was an auspicious start to a remarkable career that would include a string of popular plays, such as *Barefoot in the Park* and *The Odd Couple*, that made him the most commercially successful American comedy playwright of all time.

Norman Lear, who would go on to become one of the most influential producers in television history with hit shows such as *All in the Family* and *Maude*, also came to *Come Blow Your Horn* with a 1950s television background; his adaptation of the Simon play reflects the comic sensibilities of his early work on *The Colgate Comedy Hour* and other popular shows. Yorkin, who not only directed but also coproduced *Come Blow Your Horn* with Lear, had been a television writer-director-producer almost from the time the medium was invented, starting as a director for *The Jack Benny Program* when he was only twenty-four years old.

The impressive Simon-Lear-Yorkin trifecta, however, was not sufficient to pacify a restless Sinatra, who, true to form, pushed to do his scenes quickly and with as few takes as possible. Yorkin recalled years later that one of the few location shots in the film, a busy New York City street scene, required a lengthy set up, and by the time they were ready to shoot, Sinatra's patience with the process was all but spent. When the cameras

"You're seeing yourself for the first time, Alan. I'm just a carbon copy."

Buddy Baker to Alan Baker

Sinatra as womanizing bachelor Alan
Baker.

Sinatra and *Come Blow Your Horn*
co-star Jill St. John relax off camera.

finally rolled, Sinatra marched down the block, as the scene required, then stepped off the curb, flagged a cab, and rode away. Yorkin and crew were left standing on the sidewalk, wondering if they got the shot, and realizing that they would not get a chance to shoot it again.

Looking healthy and full of life, Sinatra bounces through *Come Blow Your Horn* with a vitality that energizes the film and easily makes his character the sympathetic favorite of the story, despite his unsavory moments. Without Sinatra's portrayal of Alan Baker, in fact, *Come Blow Your Horn* would be fairly lifeless; he's the center of the picture, even when his character is not onscreen. The screenplay was written that way by Lear, who wisely shifted the focus of the story toward Sinatra's character and away from the other Baker family members, who yell, argue, and whine with only middling comic results. The film also includes a musical number in which Sinatra's character suddenly launches into a lively version of the title song while showing Buddy around midtown Manhattan. The song is distinctly out-of-sync with the rest of the picture, but it also happens to be the best scene in the film so who's complaining?

Come Blow Your Horn was a hit both commercially and critically, and earned a Golden Globe nomination for Sinatra for Best Motion Picture Actor in a Musical or Comedy. The domestic humor of Simon's play, and the light touch Yorkin and Lear gave to the material, were precisely what Americans wanted in the summer of 1963. They liked it so much, in fact, they were willing to accept Sinatra with a new screen persona that seemed to contradict the swinger credo he had established and embodied in recent years. The voluptuous, willing females are there, as well as the stereo hi-fi and cocktails, and even the orange alpaca sweater. But styles were changing, and he was changing, too. In *Come Blow Your Horn*, domesticity suits Sinatra.

"I'm just starting my fling, Alan. You're flung."

Buddy Baker to Alan Baker

4 FOR TEXAS

A WARNER BROS. PICTURE | 1963

Director
Robert Aldrich

Screenplay
Robert Aldrich and Teddi
Sherman; W. R. Burnett
(uncredited)

Principal Cast
Frank Sinatra (Zach Thomas),
Dean Martin (Joe Jarrett), Anita
Ekberg (Elya Carlson), Ursula
Andress (Maxine Richter),
Charles Bronson (Matson), Victor
Buono (Harvey Burden)

4 FOR TEXAS is a lighthearted, lackadaisical affair, a comic western with little point except to afford Rat Pack buddies Frank Sinatra and Dean Martin an opportunity to cut up for the cameras and spend time together while getting paid for it. Playing a gambler in nineteenth-century Galveston, Texas also no doubt amused Sinatra. He did not just headline at casinos, he also owned the Cal Neva Lodge in Crystal Bay, Nevada. A hundred years earlier, a floating gambling joint like the movie's La Maison Rouge might have been his playpen.

That riverboat casino is Zach Thomas's (Sinatra) dream, but the money he was expecting to finance the enterprise ends up in the hands of rival gambler Joe Jarrett (Martin), who foils Thomas's plans when he forms a business and romantic partnership with riverboat owner Maxine Richter (Ursula Andress). Galveston's town fathers, led by banker Harvey Burden (Victor Buono), also have it in for Thomas, and are determined to put a stop to his growing power by any means necessary.

The curious thing about *4 for Texas* is that while Sinatra and Martin share equal billing and much of the action revolves around Thomas, Martin gets far more screen time, with Sinatra practically relegated to supporting-player status. No doubt director Robert Aldrich and his co-writer Teddi Sherman's screenplay went through revisions

> ## "But this money's just the beginning, Joe. If my plan works, we'll get a half a million a year."

Zach Thomas (Sinatra) trying to talk Joe Jarrett (Dean Martin) into splitting a $100,000 stagecoach payday

Zach Thomas and Joe Jarrett have an awkward first meeting as Joe prepares to make off with the $100,000 stagecoach stash.

> ## "You shoot out my eyes and I'll still find you. You put a bullet in my heart and I'll make a deal with the devil. I trade him for just enough time to come back from hell and kill you."

Hired gun Matson (Charles Bronson) letting gambler Zach Thomas know how he really feels

on set. The filmmaker was just coming off navigating warring grande dames Bette Davis and Joan Crawford through *What Ever Happened to Baby Jane?* and probably thought he was inured to star egos, but he was not prepared for Sinatra and his work habits. Their relationship deteriorated to the point that Aldrich contemplated legal action against his star for his many absences and for his negative attitude when he did report for work. According to the director's calculations, over thirty-seven days of shooting, Sinatra worked just eighty hours. No wonder Martin got all the best lines.

At least one critic noticed the star's vanishing act, as *Cinema* noted, "Sinatra worked so little that Aldrich has more shots of the back of the head of Sinatra's double than he has of Sinatra." *Variety* was equally disparaging, "Concern for the characters is never aroused by the screenplay, and the casual manner in which it is executed by the players under Aldrich's direction only compounds the problem." *Time* groused that Sinatra and Martin "appear less concerned to entertain the public than to indulge their private fantasies." *4 for Texas* fared better with the public. It scored at the box office, perhaps because as the *New York Times*'s Bosley Crowther pointed out in one of the movie's few positive reviews, "Credit Messrs. Sinatra and Martin with knowing how to live it up on the screen, to the last diamond stickpin."

Opposite top: Zach confers with duplicitous banker Harvey Burden (Victor Buono) while his bodyguard Chad (Mike Mazurki) looks on.

Opposite center: "This boat was my idea. I'm taking over as of now," Zach informs Joe just before their battle for La Maison Rouge riverboat casino begins.

Opposite bottom: With their feminine wiles and the help of a gun, Maxine Richter (Ursula Andress) and Elya Carlson (Anita Ekberg) force Joe and Zach to give up their fight and become partners.

ROBIN AND THE 7 HOODS

A WARNER BROS. PICTURE | 1964

Director
Gordon Douglas

Screenplay
David R. Schwartz

Music and lyrics
Sammy Cahn and Jimmy
Van Heusen

Principal Cast
Frank Sinatra (Robbo), Peter
Falk (Guy Gisborne), Dean Martin
(Little John), Sammy Davis, Jr.
(Will), Bing Crosby (Allen A.
Dale), Barbara Rush (Marian
Stevens), Victor Buono (Deputy
Sheriff Alvin Potts), Hank Henry
(Six Seconds), Robert Foulk
(Sheriff Octavius Glick)

THE ERA OF the original movie musical was all but over by 1963, but Warner Bros. studio head Jack Warner and Sinatra refused to believe it. So the movie titan and the movie star teamed up to produce a new musical for the screen, recruiting some of the finest musical talent in Hollywood to bring the project to life. Sammy Cahn and Jimmy Van Heusen were hired to write new songs, Nelson Riddle was enlisted to conduct the score, and Sinatra brought in his friends Sammy Davis, Jr., Dean Martin, and Bing Crosby to fill starring roles. Held together with a clever script by David R. Schwartz, *Robin and the 7 Hoods* turned out to be everything Warner and Sinatra had hoped for, though the obstacles they faced in completing it were bigger than anyone could have imagined. Some cast members wondered, in the end, how it ever got made.

The setting for *Robin and the 7 Hoods* is 1920s-era gangland Chicago, and the characters are cartoon-like hoodlums, delivering tough-guy patois as they plan assaults on their underworld competition. At the center of a crosstown rivalry are Guy Gisborne (Peter Falk), whose goal is to own every speakeasy and casino in the city, and Robbo (Sinatra), who commands a much smaller gang but runs a more popular gambling joint. Robbo is aided by his henchman, Will (Sammy Davis, Jr.), and a hustler named Little John (Dean Martin), and protected in part by the people of

> **"You stay outta the North Side. You come over there like George Washington and I'll send you back like Abe Lincoln."**
>
> ....
>
> **Robbo (Sinatra) to Guy Gisborne (Peter Falk)**

Robbo with his henchman Will (Sammy Davis, Jr.) stakes his claim to the North Side action.

> **"I'd rather keep you as an enemy, 'cause as long as I hate your guts, I know I got good taste."**
>
> ....
>
> **Robbo to Guy Gisborne**

Chicago; after Robbo inadvertently donates money to an orphanage, he becomes a media celebrity, the city's own "Robin Hood," with an entourage and fans around him wherever he goes. A fastidious do-gooder named Allen A. Dale (Bing Crosby), inspired by Robbo's generosity, joins the gang as publicist and accountant. Soon the Robin Hood image becomes a brand, with everyone from cocktail waitresses to orphanage waifs sporting green feathered caps like the legendary figure of Sherwood Forest. The gang rivalry continues throughout, but with a levity that allows hoods to easily jump into musical numbers, as when Davis sings and dances through "Bang! Bang!" or Martin plays pool while singing "Any Man Who Loves His Mother." The stars also team up for the big production numbers, "Style" and "Mr. Booze," and Sinatra delivers the musical highlight of the film when he introduces the tune "My Kind of Town."

Robin and the 7 Hoods is consistently engaging and funny, but Sinatra and his costars were smiling through extremely trying times. In November 1963, the production was filming at a Los Angeles cemetery when Sinatra, relaxing in his car between takes, heard a stunning report on the radio, and promptly told director Gordon Douglas to assemble the entire crew. To everyone working on *Robin and the 7 Hoods* that day, from actors to electricians, Sinatra delivered the news that President Kennedy had been assassinated. The group was too devastated to continue; production was shut down immediately. For Sinatra it was a personal blow, as he had known Kennedy for years and considered him a friend.

Filming resumed a few days later, but the mood had changed. Through their shared sadness and disappointment, the performers struggled to do their best and to appear lighthearted on screen. Before the cloud had lifted, just two weeks later, Sinatra received another blow: his son, Frank Sinatra, Jr., had been kidnapped at gunpoint. The nineteen-year-old Sinatra had been in Lake Tahoe, singing with his own orchestra, when kidnappers took him from his hotel room and drove off into a snowstorm. After five days he was released in exchange for ransom money, and the kidnappers were quickly caught.

> ## "I run a gamblin' joint. I hustle beer. My only aim in life is to make people happy—not croak 'em."
>
> **Robbo to Marian Stevens (Barbara Rush)**

Top: Robbo takes a shine to Little John (Dean Martin) when he realizes the lanky newcomer is hustling him in pool.

Center: Will and Robbo listen as Guy Gisborne (Peter Falk) proposes a merger.

Bottom: Guy Gisborne informs his men that he's now the underworld kingpin of Chicago.

Above: Sammy Davis, Jr. blasts his way through the "Bang! Bang!" production number.

Opposite: The rival gangs come together to celebrate the dedication of the new Chicago Police Department administration building.

Despair surrounding the production of *Robin and the 7 Hoods*, amazingly, did not prevent the top-notch cast from delivering stellar performances. Peter Falk is an amazing comic tour-de-force, using his face, hand gestures, and voice to bring Guy Gisborne to the edge of absurdity without going too far; he can't sing, but in terms of comic delivery, Falk steals the film. Bing Crosby likewise reins himself in, as when he jumps into song and dance numbers with a gentle shuffle, leaving the more exciting and less subtle moves to his younger costars. Sammy Davis, Jr., with his big solo song and dance number in the middle of the film, pulls out all the stops, and the result is a sensational set piece that rivals anything else he did on film. Sinatra even seems to be enjoying himself, as when he sings shoulder to shoulder with Crosby, the man he idolized when he was starting out in his career in the early 1940s.

The effort did not go unnoticed. "One fault of these star-studded enterprises has been that the stars frequently gave the impression that they could give only a small part of their attention and talent to the work at hand," wrote James Powers in the *Hollywood Reporter*. "*Robin and the 7 Hoods* is better than its predecessors . . . because the stars work harder." *Newsweek*'s reviewer noted that "To get the film done would have been laudable; to get it funny was heroic." The songs by Cahn and Van Heusen, so essential to the film's success, earned the team an Academy Award nomination for Best Original Song for "My Kind of Town" and a Grammy Award nomination for Best Original Motion Picture Score.

Robin and the 7 Hoods was the last movie-musical Sinatra made, and a great monument to leave behind as his career, and Hollywood, moved onto other film styles. A new idea of screen musicals was emerging, fueled in large part by pop-music films like the Beatles' *A Hard Day's Night*, released just a month and a half after *Robin and the 7 Hoods* in the summer of 1964. But Sinatra proved that great movie traditions can endure through changing times; the basic appeal of theatrical entertainment remains the same. Great jokes, songs, and dancing, he knew, would never go out of style.

Opposite top: Robbo, Allen A. Dale (Bing Crosby), and Little John deliver a musical lesson on "Style."

Opposite bottom: The gang confers with the mild-mannered Allen A. Dale (Crosby).

OTHER SINATRA FILMS
1960–1964

PEPE
A COLUMBIA PICTURE · 1960

DIRECTOR	George Sidney
SCREENPLAY	Claude Binyon and Dorothy Kingsley
STORY	Sonya Levien and Leonard Spielgass
PRINCIPAL CAST	Cantinflas (Pepe), Dan Dailey (Ted Holt), Shirley Jones (Suzie Murphy)

Sinatra makes a cameo appearance in this critically panned box-office flop starring Mexican comedian Cantinflas, who plays a peasant looking for his beloved horse in Hollywood. Playing himself in a Las Vegas sequence, Sinatra shares the screen with Cantinflas for approximately three minutes in *Pepe*.

THE ROAD TO HONG KONG
A UNITED ARTISTS RELEASE · 1962

DIRECTOR | Norman Panama

SCREENPLAY | Melvin Frank and Panama

PRINCIPAL CAST | Bing Crosby (Harry Turner), Bob Hope (Chester Babcock), Joan Collins (Diane), Robert Morley (The Leader), Dorothy Lamour (herself)

Sinatra and his "Rat Pack" crony Dean Martin pop up as cocktail-swilling astronauts in the last scene of Hope and Crosby's final "Road" film. It's an amusing throwaway bit in a labored comedy that left both audiences and critics cold.

THE LIST OF ADRIAN MESSENGER
A UNIVERSAL PICTURES RELEASE · 1963

DIRECTOR | John Huston

SCREENPLAY | Anthony Veiller
Based on the novel by Joseph MacDonald

PRINCIPAL CAST | Kirk Douglas (George Brougham), George C. Scott (Anthony Gethryn), Dana Wynter (Lady Jocelyn Bruttenholm), Clive Brook (Marquis of Gleneyre), John Merivale (Adrian Messenger)

Transforming himself into a gap-toothed gypsy, Sinatra makes a vivid cameo appearance in John Huston's mystery, which features a slew of stars (Tony Curtis, Burt Lancaster, Robert Mitchum, etc.) sporting elaborate makeup and costumes that render them unrecognizable. By all accounts, Sinatra only appears in the film's end credits, when he peels off his gypsy disguise; a double actually plays Sinatra's scene in *The List of Adrian Messenger*.

Bob Hope, Bing Crosby, Joan Collins,
Sinatra, and Dean Martin in *The Road
to Hong Kong*.

Sinatra performing one of his signature tunes.

PART 4

SINATRA'S HOLLYWOOD TWILIGHT

1965–1991

I N 1971, Frank Sinatra announced his retirement from show business and public life. The announcement began with gratitude for his "great and good fortune" and continued: "[There has been] little room or opportunity for reflection, reading, self-examination, and that need which every thinking man has for a fallow period, a long pause in which to seek a better understanding of changes occurring in the world." The latter sentence is perhaps the most revealing, suggestive of someone beginning to wonder about his own relevance to the culture at large. The years from 1965 to 1991, however, would continually test the Chairman of the Board's ability to remain on the sidelines while finding his peace.

His third wife, Mia Farrow, said she "liked Sinatra instantly," but that immediate infatuation was not enough to sustain a relationship. She resented the omnipresence of his entourage, refused to play the compliant wife, and found herself publicly humiliated when he cracked on stage that he had finally "found a broad [he could] cheat on." She filed for separation in 1967, and a year later, the couple divorced. Their marriage had lasted all of two years.

A common theme for Sinatra was that a crumbling personal life usually made for strong creative expression. In 1965, *Von Ryan's Express* premiered to critical and commercial success. The same year, his album *September of My Years* won a Grammy for Album of the Year. The career anthology that followed, *A Man and His Music,* would become Album of the Year 1966. "That's Life" and "Strangers in the Night" became *Billboard* chart toppers.

While his recording career hit new heights, Sinatra's film career languished, due to a series of critical and commercial disappointments: *Marriage on the Rocks, Assault on a Queen,* and *The Naked Runner.* He rebounded with *Tony Rome* and *The Detective,* but Sinatra's reign as a top ten box-office draw was over.

Decade's end would find him in a more contemplative frame of mind. His father died in January 1969, leaving a deeply bereaved son. According to one witness at the time, Sinatra's wreath of red roses was a simple statement of love: "Beloved Father." He disliked the '60s-era youth movement and its seeming disrespect for previous generations. American youth in turn regarded him as passé—an aging singer their parents liked. Sinatra's 1970 concept album *Watertown* sold a mere 30,000 copies and reached only 101 on the charts; as a result, plans for a television special based on the album were scrapped. So it was no wonder that in 1971 Sinatra announced his retirement and bowed out with a $250 per-person charity event for the Motion Picture and Television Relief Fund. It is somewhat telling, though, that his intended final moment, in which his silhouette was to fade into a cloud of smoke in a dimming spotlight, was undercut by calls for an encore.

Retirement did not agree with Sinatra. He continued to perform in local Palm Springs nightclubs and found himself becoming increasingly restless. In 1973, he made his official "retirement from retirement" with both a television special and an album titled *Ol' Blue Eyes is Back.* In 1974 he began touring again, but could not avoid stirring trouble. He and his entourage were implicated in several fights with casino owners and the press. Although he had answered, once and for all, any allega-

tions of *Mafiosi* connections before the House Select Committee on Crime in 1972 and acquitted himself admirably, he was continually harangued by gossip and rumor. Both the Australian and German press found themselves on the receiving end of Sinatra's biting comebacks, with the Australian press and associated unions even striking in protest until Sinatra made apologies.

Personally, he would find solace in his fourth marriage in 1976, to Barbara Marx, the ex-wife of Marx Brothers straight man, "Zeppo." The death of his mother in 1977 would see Sinatra become the calmer, quieter, more reflective person he had tried to be years earlier. He dedicated the latter half of the 1970s largely to performing in concert and to promoting charitable causes. In 1976, he was even awarded an honorary Doctorate of Humane Letters by the University of Nevada at Las Vegas.

Although he increasingly withdrew from public life, Sinatra made a rare television appearance in 1977, starring in the crime drama *Contract on Cherry Street.* Three years later, he made his first film since the critically derided comic western *Dirty Dingus Magee* (1970), playing another tough but tender gumshoe in *The First Deadly Sin* (1980).

During his ten-year absence from the big screen, Sinatra reportedly turned down roles in both *The Godfather* (1972) and *Death Wish* (1974). He had almost starred in *Dirty Harry* (1971), but a medical ailment forced him to drop out of the urban crime drama. Tepidly received by critics and audiences, *The First Deadly Sin* did not restore Sinatra to Hollywood's "A List," but it gave him one last film role worthy of his extraordinary talents. ★

*Sinatra subsequently played a cameo role in *Cannonball Run II* (1984) and appeared in the documentary *Listen Up!: The Lives of Quincy Jones* (1991).

Sinatra and his third wife, Mia
Farrow.

NONE BUT THE BRAVE

A WARNER BROS. RELEASE | 1965

Director

Frank Sinatra

Screenwriters

John Twist, Katsuya Susaki
(Kikumaru Okuda, story)

Principal Cast

Tatsuya Mihashi (Lt. Kuroki),
Takeshi Kato (Sgt. Tamura), Clint
Walker (Capt. Dennis Bourke),
Tommy Sands (2nd Lt. Blair),
Brad Dexter (Sgt. Bleaker), Tony
Bill (Air Crewman Keller), Frank
Sinatra (Chief Pharmacist Mate
Francis Malloy)

"THE BRAVE ARE NEVER different—only different looking!" blared the tagline for *None But the Brave*, Frank Sinatra's sole directing effort. Not exactly a subtle line for a movie in which American and Japanese soldiers share an island during World War II, but it quickly got the point across that this was not the usual war drama. Still very much a liberal at this time, Sinatra found a property in which he could make more than a film—he could make a statement.

An aerial dogfight leads to an American plane crash landing on a small South Pacific island. The GIs who survive the crash quickly realize they are not alone. A Japanese battalion is similarly stranded. Skirmishes diminish the numbers on both sides until a wounded soldier, Lance Cpl. Hirano (Homare Suguro), develops gangrene. With no medic in his camp, the Japanese superior officer Lt. Kuroki (Tatsuya Mihashi) approaches the Americans for help and Chief Pharmacist Mate Francis Malloy (Sinatra) answers the call. The experience impresses both Kuroki and American commander Capt. Bourke (Clint Walker) so much that they declare a truce over the objections of their hotheaded junior officers, 2nd Lt. Blair (Tommy Sands) and Sgt. Tamura (Takeshi Kato). But the men also agree that if either side is able to establish communication with the outside world and call for help, the battle will resume.

> **"The toughest thing I had to do on the first day of shooting was to say 'Print.' It took me ten minutes, because I liked the take, but I figured the minute I say 'print,' I'm on the record."**

Frank Sinatra on his introduction to directing

Chief Pharmacist Mate Francis Malloy inspects precious cargo soon after his platoon crash lands on a South Pacific island.

> **"I'm a Band-Aid man. I'm not a surgeon. I put mercurochrome on the scratches of the guys."**

Chief Pharmacist Mate Malloy (Sinatra) offering a frank assessment of his skills to Lt. Kuroki (Tatsuya Mihashi)

Above: The auteur speaks: Sinatra explains the themes of his directorial film debut, *None But the Brave.*

Opposite top: Malloy and Captain Dennis Bourke (Clint Walker) inform officious 2nd Lt. Blair (Tommy Sands) that in the wake of their plane crash, his precious rules and regulations no longer apply.

Opposite center: Cpl. Craddock (Sammy Jackson) and Capt. Bourke (Richard Bakalyan) lead the way on a mission through the jungle.

Opposite bottom: Sgt. Bleeker (Brad Dexter), Malloy, Cpl. Ruffino, Capt. Bourke, and 2nd Lt. Blair lay their fallen comrades to rest.

Based on a story by Kikumaru Okuda and adapted for the screen by John Twist and Katsuya Susaki, the film is diligent in granting equal weight to the American and Japanese viewpoints. That *None But the Brave* intends to provide a different way of looking at World War II is evident from opening credits in both languages. Dialogue, too, is bilingual with subtitled Japanese. Only Kuroki, who also spins the tale in a heavily accented English-language voiceover narration, speaks both tongues.

Too much of the dialogue in either language is tin-eared, and with the exception of the boozy, cynical Malloy and thoughtful, empathetic Kuroki, the characters are little more than ciphers. Too often, the acting, especially on the American side, also falters. Sinatra and Mihashi (a costar of Akira Kurosawa's *The Bad Sleep Well* and *High and Low*) are terrific and so is Richard Bakalyan as tough Cpl. Ruffino, but most of the performances are overly broad. The worst offender is Sands, Sinatra's then son-in-law, reportedly cast at daughter Nancy's urging. He delivers a turn so jarringly cartoonish that the movie stops dead every time he is onscreen.

Those missteps aside, *None But the Brave* offers not just a unique viewing experience but also a window into Sinatra's worldview as he approached his fiftieth birthday. On the surface, the film was standard Hollywood fare, but it was also ahead of its time. At the dawn of the Vietnam era, Sinatra was prescient, mounting an unapologetic antiwar film that anticipated the sentiments that would sweep America's youth and roil the country in the near future. In emphasizing the Japanese point of view and giving voice to people typically portrayed as the enemy, *None But the Brave* also presaged by nearly forty years Clint Eastwood's thematically similar epic, *Letters from Iwo Jima* (2006).

Sinatra nearly missed the opportunity to direct the movie, a coproduction partnering the star's own Sinatra Enterprises with Warner Bros. and Japan's Toho Film. Warner Bros. objected to putting the film in the hands of a neophyte, but Sinatra's executive producer and business partner Howard W. Koch made a winning plea on his behalf. Though Sinatra would never attempt the feat again, he seemed to enjoy the experience.

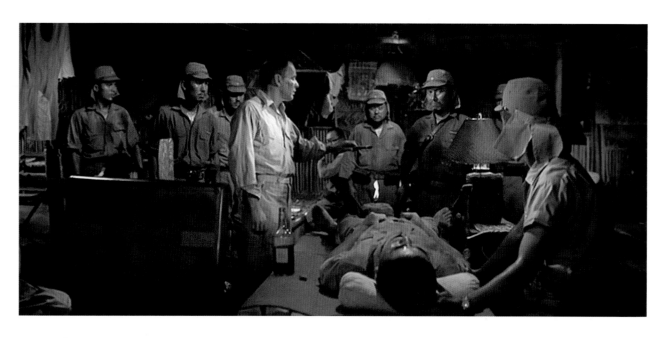

For one thing, the restless entertainer discovered that directing was so time consuming that he never became bored. Sinatra also appreciated the challenge, as he explained to *New York Times* reporter Peter Bart: "I found out that it was in some ways tougher than I had thought. The director has so many things to worry about—pace, wardrobe, performance. . . . Next time, I won't try to perform when I direct."

Sinatra substituted Hawaii for his unnamed South Pacific Isle and he nearly died there during *None But the Brave*'s production, when he got caught in a fierce undertow at Kauai's Nawiliwili Bay. Enjoying a break from filming at the beach near Lihue, he got into trouble when he swam out to save Koch's wife, Ruth, from drowning. She made it back to land; he didn't. Sinatra struggled in the waves 200 yards offshore for thirty-five minutes. His friend and costar Brad Dexter rushed to his side, as did a group of locals. They were finally able to get him back to shore, but it was a close call, as Lihue fire lieutenant George Keawe related, "In another five minutes, he would have been gone. His face was turning blue."

Sinatra might have wished he had drowned when he read *None But the Brave*'s reviews. They were not all terrible. *Variety* praised his skill at "maintaining a suspenseful pace." But the reviews that were bad were downright vicious. *Time* magazine declared, "The idea holds some promise, except that Director Sinatra and his scriptwriters goof away tension at every turn." The *New York Times*' Bosley Crowther dripped with contempt for Sinatra from his review's opening sentences: "If the threat of Frank Sinatra as a film director is judged by his first try on *None But the Brave*, it is clear that there need be no apprehension among the members of the Screen Directors Guild. A minimum show of creative invention and a maximum use of cinema clichés are evident in the staging of this war film."

With notices like that, perhaps it is not surprising that Sinatra never directed again. And it no doubt stung that after *None But the Brave*'s modest box office, his *other* 1965 World War II movie, the Mark Robson-directed *Von Ryan's Express,* became one of his biggest movie successes.

Opposite top: Malloy hands Sgt. Tamura (Takeshi Kato) a blade to sterilize as he prepares to operate on Lance Cpl. Hirano (Homare Suguro).

Opposite center: With little cover, Cpl. Ruffino, 2nd Lt. Blair, Malloy, Capt. Bourke, and Sgt. Bleeker make a stand against the enemy.

Opposite bottom: A brief moment of rest in the action of *None But the Brave.*

Sinatra makes tough calls as the
director of *None But the Brave*.

Sinatra calls the shots.

VON RYAN'S EXPRESS

A TWENTIETH CENTURY-FOX PICTURE | 1965

Director

Mark Robson

Screenplay

Wendell Mayes and Joseph
Landon

Based on the novel by David
Westheimer

Principal Cast

Frank Sinatra (Col. Joseph L.
Ryan), Trevor Howard (Maj. Eric
Fincham), Brad Dexter (Sgt.
Bostick), Sergio Fantoni (Capt.
Oriani), Adolfo Celi (Maj.
Battaglia), Raffaella Carra
(Gabriella), Richard Bakalyan
(Cpl. Giannini), James Brolin
(Pvt. Ames), Edward Mulhare
(Capt. Costanzo)

FRANK SINATRA MADE war pictures throughout his career, but only one, *Von Ryan's Express*, was a true action film, with Sinatra as the action hero who thinks on his feet, moves fast, and scrambles from one tight spot to the next. The film is a World War II drama that casts Sinatra as a military leader once again, but this time he's a flawed character, making as many bad decisions as good ones and scrambling to keep his men moving as they resist his orders and curse his name. Once the film gets moving, the excitement and suspense are nonstop, with no breaks in the action where Sinatra's character can get cozy with a female character or a bottle of booze.

Von Ryan's Express begins with the crash landing of American Col. Joseph Ryan's plane in central Italy, and his prompt incarceration in an Italian fascist-run POW camp. Ryan is the ranking officer among the prisoners, but from the start he butts heads with British Maj. Eric Fincham (Trevor Howard), who believes Ryan misunderstands everything about their predicament, especially their plans to escape. Ryan orders the men to stay put until the Allies liberate the camp, but he's forced to act when the fascists fall from power and the Nazis start to move in. Along with a sympathetic Italian officer, Capt. Oriani (Sergio Fantoni), the POWS are quickly captured and loaded onto a Nazi train, but Ryan and Fincham orchestrate a takeover by killing the Nazi soldiers on board and taking

"**You'd better know what you're doing—unless you want a mutiny on your hands.**"

Maj. Eric Fincham (Trevor Howard) to Col. Joseph L. Ryan (Sinatra)

"**You'll get your Iron Cross now, 'Von' Ryan!**"

Maj. Eric Fincham to Col. Joseph L. Ryan

"**A bird-colonel outranks a bird-brain, clear?**"

Col. Joseph L. Ryan to Private Ame (James Brolin)

Left: From their first encounter, Colonel Ryan and Major Fincham (Trevor Howard) are at odds about how best to protect their fellow POWs.

Right: Despite tensions on the set, Trevor Howard claimed to have enjoyed working with Sinatra. *Von Ryan's Express* was a major critical and commercial hit.

their uniforms. Only one member of their group speaks German, Capt. Costanzo (Edward Mulhare), so he pretends to be the leader whenever the train goes through Nazi checkpoints, where he converses sternly and convincingly with Nazi station agents and police.

Ryan and his comrades improvise their way through a series of riveting encounters, as when a Gestapo notices Ryan's American-made watch and tries to barter for it; he offers nylons and cigarettes while Ryan, who doesn't understand German, negotiates the deal without speaking a word. But the Nazis running the railroad lines soon realize that one of their trains is not traveling on designated routes, and it dawns on them quickly that Ryan and company are making a run for the Swiss border. The chase is on, and Ryan, dubbed "Von" Ryan as a sign of disrespect from the men he commands, barks orders and reverses them in a desperate attempt to move his troops to safety with impulsive decisions that are always bold and often fatal. The tension continues right up to the surprise ending, a dramatic twist added at Sinatra's insistence and vastly different from the cheerful conclusion of its source material, David Westheimer's 1964 novel.

There was drama behind the scenes as well. While *Von Ryan's Express* was filming on location in rural Italy, Sinatra's ex-wife Ava Gardner was working on *The Bible . . . In the Beginning* (1966) in Rome, and there was still enough affection between them to merit a reunion, or at least a few dinners with a few rounds of drinks. Their once volatile relationship had simmered down, but the meetings were not lighthearted either, both parties appeared to be worn down by years of animosity and anguish, much of it publicly displayed. The meetings with Gardner left Sinatra frustrated, and his mood on the set wasn't much better, as the filming process took more time than he cared to give. Sinatra focused his impatience on director Mark Robson, and the two clashed repeatedly.

Back in Los Angeles to shoot *Von Ryan's Express* interiors on a Twentieth Century-Fox soundstage, Sinatra's mood brightened when nineteen-year-old Mia Farrow paid a visit to the set. A star of the television series *Peyton Place*, also filmed on the Fox lot, Farrow was well known

in Hollywood circles as the daughter of director John Farrow and actress Maureen O'Sullivan; in fact, Sinatra had met her before, when she was a child. This time the sparks flew, and within a day Farrow had flown off for a rendezvous with Sinatra at his Palm Springs home. Sinatra was fifty years old when the relationship began, a fact that was reported relentlessly when the couple went public, but friends of Sinatra were more concerned with the difference in the couple's outlook and experience—the fact that Farrow was more hippie than hip. The pairing was also complicated by the fact that Gardner had once dated Farrow's father, and Mia was younger than two of Sinatra's children. Still, it was more than a fling, and they proved it over time. After more than a year and a half together, Sinatra and Farrow were married.

Von Ryan's Express was an enormous success. Though he had proven his skill in many genres, the part of commander and action hero struck many as the best possible fit for him, and reviews were among the most glowing in his career. "Sinatra's expertly done Von Ryan is a harsh character," wrote Thomas Thompson in *Life*. "It is a role that calls for nuances that Sinatra has rarely had to express before." Abe Greenberg, in the Hollywood *Citizen-News* noted that Sinatra "underplays his role neatly and purposefully where it might lead him into an overdramatic trap . . . This is Sinatra at his best as an actor."

A new era in action movies was still a few years off, with films like *Bullitt* (1968) and *The French Connection* (1971) establishing the pervasive thrill-ride style that became the genre's norm. But Sinatra was ahead of the trend, and the innovative pacing of *Von Ryan's Express* is one of the reasons it continues to be heralded as one of his best pictures. With just a few years' experience as a producer, Sinatra's eye for good material had become sharper, and he spotted a piece that might otherwise have been overlooked. After reading Westheimer's novel, Sinatra learned that Twentieth Century-Fox owned the rights to *Von Ryan's Express*, so he promptly informed the studio that he was ready to play Ryan. It was a shrewd maneuver that paid off, both critically and commercially.

Opposite top: While his men rest, Ryan considers the next move in his cross-country escape plan.

Opposite center: Disguised as German soldiers, Ryan, Captain Costanzo (Edward Mulhare), and Major Fincham prepare to face the Gestapo in a Nazi-controlled train station.

Opposite bottom: On top of a fast-moving train, Ryan crawls toward an unsuspecting Nazi guard.

MARRIAGE ON THE ROCKS

A TWENTIETH CENTURY-FOX PICTURE | 1965

Director

Jack Donohue

Screenplay

Cy Howard

Principal Cast

Frank Sinatra (Dan Edwards),
Dean Martin (Ernie Brewer),
Deborah Kerr (Valerie Edwards),
Nancy Sinatra (Tracy
Edwards), Cesar Romero (Miguel
Santos), Hermione Baddeley
(Jeannie MacPherson), Tony Bill
(Jim Blake), John McGiver
(Shad Nathan), Davey Davison
(Lisa Sterling), Michael Petit
(David Edwards)

MARRIAGE ON THE ROCKS represented the end of an era for Rat Pack pals Frank Sinatra and Dean Martin. The battle-of-the-sexes comedy marked the last time that the two Rat Pack pals would truly share the screen. They would appear one more time together (along with their confederate Sammy Davis, Jr.) when Sinatra made a cameo appearance in 1984's lamentable *Cannonball Run II. Marriage on the Rocks* was a final moment for the pair to star side by side, as two sides of an accidental love triangle with Deborah Kerr.

Cast against type as an uptight square, Sinatra plays ad man Dan Edwards, who plans to sit home watching TV on his wedding anniversary, explaining to his easygoing best friend Ernie Brewer (Martin), "I don't have to be romantic; I'm married." His wife, Valerie (Kerr), is so sick of that attitude that she contemplates divorce. At Ernie's suggestion, the couple travel to Mexico for a second honeymoon, a trip that opens the door to a comedy of errors that ends with Dan taking the role of the swinging bachelor, while Ernie becomes Val's uptight husband.

For Sinatra, making *Marriage on the Rocks* turned out to be a true family affair when his eldest child Nancy came on board to play Dan's teenage daughter Tracy. She was thrilled to work alongside her father, but she later wrote, "I was still *very* nervous. And, of course, I felt the

"Does this look like an apron?" Valerie Edwards demands of husband Dan and pal Ernie Brewer.

> "I want a divorce, Shad, D-I-V-O-R-C-E, on the grounds of boredom, just plain boredom."
>
> Valerie Edwards (Deborah Kerr) to lawyer Shad Nathan (John McGiver) on her nineteenth wedding anniversary

> "Dan's become a square. Remember what a swinger he was when we were kids?"
>
> Valerie venting her frustrations to Ernie (Dean Martin)

added pressure of wanting my dad to be proud of me." The experience turned out to be a bittersweet one for the younger Sinatra when in the middle of the production her husband, Tommy Sands, left her.

Sinatra's *From Here to Eternity* costar Kerr had reservations about doing the movie, but Sinatra and her friend David Niven convinced her to take the part. Nicknamed "the Jolly Green Giant" by her shorter co-stars Sinatra and Martin after they caught sight of her costumed in green chiffon, she enjoyed her time on the set. "It was so much fun, a joke, and all quite ludicrous," she remembered. "Frank would come in one morning and say, 'We don't need this scene!' and just tear it out of the script and throw it away."

By the time *Marriage on the Rocks* came out in September 1965, Sinatra's complicated love life was again gossip column fodder as he romanced actress Mia Farrow, thirty years his junior. The marital shenanigans in the movie paled in comparison and critics were not kind. *Time* magazine's dismal assessment: "The befuddled trio runs into plot complications so dreary that mother-in-law Hermione Baddeley has to march drunkenly around the premises, tootling a bagpipe at intervals to keep everyone awake." On that sorry note, the Rat Pack movie era faded out.

*"**Marriage on the Rocks** is the most recent effort to capture for posterity the fanny-pinching sophistication of Dean Martin and Frank Sinatra."*

Time

Opposite top: While Dan broods, Valerie makes the most of her second honeymoon in Mexico, cutting a rug with lawyer Miguel Santos (Cesar Romero).

Opposite bottom: New bachelor Dan shows off his moves with gal pal Lisa (Davey Davison) at the Café a Go Go.

ASSAULT ON A QUEEN

A PARAMOUNT PICTURES RELEASE | 1966

Director
Jack Donohue

Screenplay
Rod Serling

Based on the novel by Jack Finney

Principal Cast
Frank Sinatra (Mark Brittain), Virna Lisi (Rosa Lucchesi), Anthony Franciosa (Vic Rossiter), Richard Conte (Tony Moreno), Alf Kjellin (Eric Lauffnauer), Errol John (Linc Langley)

THE SECOND TIME was not the charm for Sinatra and *Marriage on the Rocks* director Jack Donohue, who reteamed to middling effect on *Assault on a Queen*. Based on Jack Finney's 1959 novel, this aquatic heist yarn is a standard-issue potboiler that meanders to its anticlimax of an ending. For all its flaws, however, *Assault on a Queen* remains palatable, primarily because of Sinatra's chemistry with leading lady Virna Lisi, a Neapolitan bombshell who appeared in a handful of American films in the 1960s.

A Sinatra Enterprises production, *Assault on a Queen* unfolds in the sparkling waters off the Bahamas, where World War II veteran Mark Brittain (Sinatra) ekes out a living as a charter boat fisherman. Against his better judgment, he takes a job as a deep-sea diver for a trio of treasure hunters: Italian beauty Rosa Lucchesi (Lisi), her snake of an erstwhile boyfriend Vic Rossiter (Anthony Franciosa), and former German U-boat commander Eric Lauffnauer (Alf Kjellin). What begins as a search for a legendary sunken Spanish galleon turns into a highly improbable plan to rob the *Queen Mary*. Mark discovers an *intact* German submarine on the ocean floor. Raising and retrofitting the submarine with the help of Moreno (Richard Conte) and Mark's Bahamian sidekick Linc (Errol John), the "pirates" will use a dummy torpedo to intimidate the liner's captain into letting them board the Queen Mary and steal $1 million in gold.

> ## "Me stick up the Queen Mary? Lady, you're off your rocker!"
>
> ···
>
> **Assault on a Queen poster**

> ## "I live my life as I see fit . . . and I have a ball."
>
> ···
>
> Mark Brittain (Sinatra)

> ## "If you're so difficult now, Mr. Brittain, how can we ever become friends?"
>
> ···
>
> Rosa Lucchesi (Virna Lisi) to Brittain

Left: Sinatra enjoyed working with Italian actress Virna Lisi, who made a handful of American films in the 1960s.

Right: Sinatra as Mark Brittain.

THEY
STICK
UP THE
QUEEN
MARY
IN MID
ATLANTIC

QUEEN MARY

PARAMOUNT PICTURES in association with SEVEN ARTS and SINATRA ENTERPRISES presents

FRANK **SINATRA** VIRNA **LISI** in

ASSAULT ON A QUEEN

He's an I've-tried-everything guy.
She's an I'll-try-anything girl.

CO-STARRING
Richard **CONTE** · Errol **JOHN** · Alf **KJELLIN** and TONY **FRANCIOSA** AS "ROSSITER"

TECHNICOLOR®
PANAVISION®

Screenplay by ROD SERLING · From the novel by JACK FINNEY · Produced by WILLIAM GOETZ · Directed by JACK DONOHUE

Despite festering tensions between Mark and Vic over Rosa, the daring heist goes according to plan—until Vic's greed puts them all in harm's way.

Although the *New York Times*'s Bosley Crowther criticized Sinatra's "bland assurance" in *Assault on a Queen*, the star's relaxed, unflappable performance holds up far better than Franciosa's scenery-chewing turn as the craven Rossiter. There's a matter-of-fact confidence to Sinatra's acting, especially in his scenes with Lisi, who adds much needed "oomph" to a largely decorative role. Granted, their romance develops along fairly predictable lines, but Sinatra and Lisi have a natural rapport that transcends the rote quality of Rod Serling's frustratingly pedestrian screenplay. Apparently the stars got along well off-screen, as Tom Santopietro relates in *Sinatra in Hollywood*. Asked about his gorgeous costar, Sinatra quipped, "If they'd had Virna in the Mafia, I'd never have torn up my membership card."

Sadly, there's nothing as memorable as Sinatra's one-liner in *Assault on a Queen*, which lacks a crucial sense of dramatic urgency—an impression compounded by Duke Ellington's incongruous jazz score. The film's tenuous-at-best narrative credibility is further undermined by the obvious process shots and embarrassing use of miniatures; the submarine scenes look as if they were filmed in the producer's swimming pool.

Panned by critics, *Assault on a Queen* tanked at the box office, just like Sinatra's prior collaboration with Donohue, *Marriage on the Rocks*. Suffice to say, they did not work together again.

Opposite: The poster for *Assault on a Queen* promised more than it delivered.

Below: Director Jack Donohue, Sinatra and famed restaurant owner Michael Romanoff relax on the set of *Assault on a Queen*.

THE NAKED RUNNER

A WARNER BROS. PICTURES RELEASE | 1967

Director
Sidney J. Furie

Screenplay
Stanley Mann

Based on the novel by Francis
Clifford

Principal Cast
Frank Sinatra (Sam Laker), Peter
Vaughan (Slattery), Derren
Nesbitt (Col. Hartmann), Nadia
Gray (Karen), Toby Robins
(Ruth), Inger Stratton (Anna),
Edward Fox (Ritchie Jackson),
Michael Newport (Patrick Laker)

SINATRA'S MID-1960S run of critical and commercial disappoint-ments continued with *The Naked Runner*, a Cold War-era espionage film that suffers from a near-fatal lack of narrative momentum and dramatic intrigue. Savaged by critics at the time of its release, Sidney J. Furie's adaptation of Francis Clifford's 1966 novel begins promisingly, with a taut first act that's closer in spirit to John Le Carré than James Bond. But an exposition-heavy screenplay, combined with a nearly monochromatic visual palette, gradually drains the energy from *The Naked Runner*. Sina-tra, however, gives an effective performance that holds up far better than the film. Hailed as a "grand, strong thriller" by mystery writer Anthony Boucher in the *New York Times*, Clifford's novel certainly has all the ingredients to make a gripping, austerely realistic espionage yarn.

Sinatra portrays Sam Laker, a widowed American industrialist living in London with his young son, Patrick (Michael Newport). Scheduled to attend a trade show in East Germany, Sam receives a surprise call from British intelligence officer Martin Slattery (Peter Vaughan), who had worked alongside Sam, a former O.S.S. officer and expert marksman, during World War II. Would Sam consider taking a message to his old flame, agent Karen Gisevius (Nadia Gray), in Leipzig? Wary yet anxious to reconnect with Karen, Sam reluctantly agrees to help Slattery. What

> **"They found the key to Sam Laker.
> They wound it up good and tight.
> And then they turned him loose."**
>
> ....
>
> *The Naked Runner* tagline

> **"Not only British Intelligence, but
> anybody's intelligence, is likely to
> be affronted by this potboiler."**
>
> ....
>
> *Variety*

Left: Sinatra as Sam Laker, the American industrialist forced to assassinate a political defector, in *The Naked Runner*.

Right: Sam Laker takes expert aim.

appears to be a simple errand turns out to be a ploy by Slattery, who wants Sam to carry out a far more dangerous assignment: assassinate a freed political prisoner before he reveals state secrets to the Kremlin. If Sam refuses, the ruthless East German secret police officer, Colonel Hartmann (Derren Nesbit), will kill Patrick.

After working with the journeyman director Jack Donohue on the back-to-back flops *Marriage on the Rocks* and *Assault on a Queen*, Sinatra teamed with the red-hot Furie, who'd scored a hit with *The Ipcress File* (1966), the first of three Harry Palmer spy films starring Michael Caine as the scruffy alternative to 007. And fresh from cowriting the Academy-Award nominated screenplay for *The Collector* (1965), Stanley Mann was hired to adapt Clifford's novel. So how did they miss the mark so completely with *The Naked Runner*?

The production was partly hobbled by Sinatra's "anywhere but here" attitude toward location filming. Not only did he stop production to jet off to Las Vegas to marry Mia Farrow, he later took off for California to campaign for Governor Edmund Brown. His behavior reportedly infuriated Furie, who had to use a double for certain scenes because Sinatra refused to return to the film's set in Copenhagen.

That said, Sinatra cannot be held responsible for the film's mediocrity. Furie's monotonous visual style—slate gray color scheme, excessive use of tight close-ups—and Mann's laboriously talky screenplay prevent *The Naked Runner* from realizing the potential of its first act. What works is Sinatra's tightly wound performance as Laker. He may have played the petulant, entitled star to the hilt off-camera, holding up production and demanding to be helicoptered to locations, but onscreen, Sinatra delivers the goods in *The Naked Runner*.

Above: Sam en route to his fateful appointment in Leipzig.

Opposite top: Sam and his young son Patrick (Michael Newport) in their sleek, ultra-modern London flat.

Opposite bottom: Sam in the crosshairs.

TONY ROME

A TWENTIETH CENTURY-FOX PICTURE | 1967

Director
Gordon Douglas

Screenplay
Richard Breen

Principal Cast
Frank Sinatra (Tony Rome), Jill St. John (Ann Archer), Richard Conte (Lt. Dave Santini), Gena Rowlands (Rita Kosterman), Simon Oakland (Rudy Kosterman), Jeffrey Lynn (Adam Boyd), Robert J. Wilke (Ralph Turpin), Diana (Sue Lyon), Lloyd Bochner (Vic Rood)

ONCE FRANK SINATRA found out how neatly he fit into the role of a private detective, it was practically all he wanted to do on film. Four of his last five leading roles were in detective films, starting with *Tony Rome*, a film that bridges the film noir style of twenty years earlier with the mod mindset of the Lyndon Johnson era. Audiences liked the idea too—Sinatra as a tough guy who's tender with the ladies; the world-weary pragmatist with a glimmer of hope; the cat too cool for rock 'n' roll, bucking the trends with his dark suit and fedora; and a fellow too busy to commit to a woman, but always with a minute to spare for a beer or martini. In many ways the character Sinatra was playing on screen was the man his fans already imagined him to be.

Tony Rome casts Sinatra as the title character, a Miami gumshoe who lives on his boat, drives a beat-up convertible, and supports himself mostly by gambling. He's a retired Miami police detective who's kept up his connections, so when a case falls into his lap he has everyone from insurance inspectors to morgue attendants ready to lend a hand. The intrigue in *Tony Rome* begins with a young woman named Diana (Sue Lyon) who's been found passed out drunk in a hotel, and Rome is called in by his former partner, now the hotel security, to get her home without incident. It's a simple chore that leads him further into a

Ann Archer entertains Rome on her living-room floor.

> **"I'm warning you, no heavy-duty stuff. If it is, I'm just passing through."**
>
> ....
>
> Tony Rome (Sinatra) to Ralph Turpin (Robert J. Wilke)

> **"Up to now I haven't found a dame who's a bookmaker. See, I gamble. And that wouldn't be a nice life for a lady. Besides that I live on a boat and I like it."**
>
> ....
>
> Tony Rome to Ann Archer (Jill St. John)

dysfunctional family and a smorgasbord of criminal activity. The young woman hires Rome to find her missing jewelry; her ultra-wealthy father, Rudy Kosterman (Simon Oakland), hires Rome to find out why his daughter is acting strangely; and Kosterman's wife, Rita (Gena Rowlands), engages Rome to keep certain information a secret from her husband. In the Kosterman mansion, Rome meets Ann Archer (Jill St. John), a party guest left over from the previous night. Archer tells Rome that pickings are slim and she'll settle for him, and Rome agrees to give it a shot, but only after the mysteries are solved. As the Kosterman case expands to include murder, blackmail, and kidnapping, Rome sleuths around the city collecting clues from a variety of hoodlums and miscreants. Between near-death experiences, Rome has a few cocktails with Archer, and swings by the Kosterman place to lay it on the line: He knows that all this mayhem can be traced to Kosterman family secrets, and he intends to find out exactly what they are.

Tony Rome borrows lightly from Humphrey Bogart films such as *The Maltese Falcon* (1941) and *The Big Sleep* (1946), and Sinatra did admire Bogart and counted him as a friend. But the film and the character of Tony Rome are far too modern to be considered a serious homage to Bogart, and only the structure, a rambling mystery that spins out to include multiple subplots and characters, bears any resemblance to the film-noir style. For the most part, the action in *Tony Rome* takes place in bright Miami sunshine, with Rome's dark suit and shoes the only colorless objects on display.

Jill St. John is the opposite of a femme fatale, a harmless, cheerful party girl who wants nothing more from Rome than a chance to cuddle and coo before he dashes off again. In fact, *Tony Rome* bears more resemblance to the television detective series that pervaded the airwaves in the 1970s and '80s, such as *The Rockford Files* and *Baretta*. Like those programs, *Tony Rome* features a maverick content to lead a low-rent bachelor lifestyle, a hotheaded police friend who blows up when the rules are bent, wisecracks for any occasion, eccentric friends, and a parade of pretty women who interest the private eye, but not as much as the case he's on.

Above: Rome's brother-in-law, Lt. Dave Santini (Richard Conte) of the Miami police, sends him on his way after an interrogation session.

Opposite top: Ann Archer warms up to Tony Rome while detailing the tedium of her party-girl lifestyle.

Opposite center: Shifting through his ransacked boat, Rome wonders why he ever got involved with Diana (Sue Lyon).

Opposite bottom: Rome in his low-rent office.

But *Tony Rome* is many notches above run-of-the-mill television drama. While Sinatra is the main reason, brilliant actors such as Gena Rowlands and Richard Conte, and the charming Jill St. John, also contributed greatly to the film's success.

Moviegoers made *Tony Rome* a hit when it opened in November 1967, but reviews were mixed, with many critics unwilling to accept Sinatra as a detective simply because of the history of privates eyes on film. "That Sinatra is no Bogart is hardly news," *Time* magazine noted coldly, and Bosley Crowther of the *New York Times* faulted Sinatra for coming up with a "callous, cool-cat character somewhat short of old Bogey's." Others made the same comparison, but delivered it as a compliment, such as Hollis Alpert of the *Saturday Review*: "*Tony Rome* is lively and entertaining," wrote Alpert, "and for this we must thank both the capable Mr. Sinatra and the persistent ghost of Mr. Bogart. . . . Frank Sinatra has been a talent in search of a role ever since *The Manchurian Candidate*, and at last, in *Tony Rome*, he has found himself one."

At a time when Sinatra had the power and popularity to make any kind of film he wanted, he chose to keep a good thing going and make more films in the *Tony Rome* mold. Now in his fifties, he was slowly stepping away from the swinger persona, and instead embracing the middle-aged cool of a man who's still hip and virile but wouldn't be caught dead in a Nehru jacket and love beads.

Top: Rome waits for Ann Archer.

Center: Rome informs Rudy Kosterman (Simon Oakland) of the latest twist in the case.

Bottom: Rome saves millionaire Rudy Kosterman from assassins.

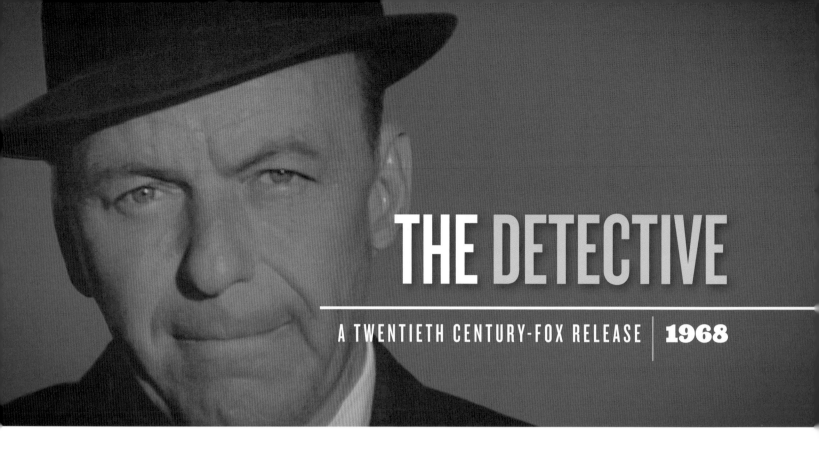

THE DETECTIVE

A TWENTIETH CENTURY-FOX RELEASE | 1968

Director
Gordon Douglas

Screenplay
Abby Mann

Based on the novel by
Roderick Thorp

Principal Cast
Frank Sinatra (Detective Sgt. Joe Leland), Lee Remick (Karen Wagner Leland), Ralph Meeker (Curran), Al Freeman, Jr. (Robbie), Robert Duvall (Nestor), Jack Klugman (Dave Schoenstein), Lloyd Bochner (Dr. Wendell Roberts), Horace McMahon (Capt. Tom Farrell), Tony Musante (Felix Tesla), Jacqueline Bisset (Norma MacIver)

AT A TIME WHEN wholesome, big-budget movie musicals were dominating the box office, a new type of American cinema was emerging and Frank Sinatra, as usual, was ahead of the trend. Gritty urban realism was edging its way into mainstream motion pictures, hastening the demise of the Production Code, which had long forced filmmakers to tiptoe around certain subjects. Although audiences were still lining up to see family-friendly musicals like *Oliver!* (1968) and *Chitty Chitty Bang Bang* (1968), they were also turning out in droves for such envelope-pushing films as *The Boston Strangler* (1968) and Sinatra's *The Detective*, a police drama that depicts the taboo subject of homosexuality with a candor rare in 1960s-era American cinema.

In Abby Mann's adaptation of Roderick Thorp's 1966 bestseller, Sinatra plays New York City police detective Joe Leland, a seasoned veteran who is blasé about all manner of atrocities, but not so jaded that he's stopped caring about innocent people in difficult circumstances. He investigates homicides methodically, treating socialites and junkies with equal respect, and only loses his cool when he catches his fellow cops stepping outside the law. While investigating the savage murder of a wealthy gay man, Leland is appalled by the blatant homophobia of fellow cops Robbie (Al Freeman, Jr.) and Nestor (Robert Duvall), who

> **"I don't know what's gonna happen to me. Maybe the same thing that happened to my old man—I'll wind up on a scrap heap."**
>
> ·····················
>
> **Joe Leland (Sinatra) to Capt. Tom Farrell (Horace McMahon)**

> **"I don't get this loner thing. Your old man was never that way. You know, with Karen you were more of a human being."**
>
> ·····················
>
> **Capt. Tom Farrell to Joe Leland**

New York City police detective Joe Leland and fellow officer Nestor (Robert Duvall) at the scene of a brutal murder.

Joe Leland meets his future wife Karen (Lee Remick) on the dance floor at a university social.

"It's what I do best. It's my life. And it's worth something!"

Joe Leland to Karen Wagner Leland (Lee Remick)

think nothing of roughing up innocent gay men. Not that Leland always walks the moral high ground; his interrogation of the prime suspect, the victim's mentally fragile ex-roommate Felix Tesla (Tony Musante), elicits a false confession that ultimately sends an innocent man to the electric chair.

The case is officially pronounced closed, but that changes after Leland receives a visit from a young widow, Norma MacIver (Jacqueline Bisset), whose husband died under mysterious circumstances. With the help of his one ally on the squad, Dave Schoenstein (Jack Klugman), Leland delves into the MacIver case. What he uncovers not only solves the murder but also exposes a vast network of corruption involving city politicians, real estate developers, and members of Leland's own squad.

The parallel story in *The Detective*, an intimate look at Leland's personal life, is also downbeat in tone. In a series of flashbacks, we see the meeting between Leland and future wife, Karen (Lee Remick), their happy courtship, and the difficult married life that hits Leland harder than anything he's experiencing on the job. He can handle Karen's cursory interest in all things trendy (she enjoys "new theater" and lectures on

Top: Joe takes a break from an evening of "new theater."

Center: Karen drops into the police station to tell Joe she's fallen for him.

Bottom: Joe proposes to Karen in the grandstands at a New York Jets game

LSD) but her admission that she's a nymphomaniac with multiple part-ners is more than the no-nonsense detective can bear.

In *The Detective* Sinatra was surrounded by talented up-and-coming stars of the time. Robert Duvall had worked steadily as a character actor on television, but his career was shifting to feature films; his appearance in *The Detective* was followed by a leading role in *True Grit* the following year. Jack Klugman, who had also labored in near-obscurity on the small screen, was only a few years away from becoming a household name with his performance as Oscar Madison on the long-running television sitcom *The Odd Couple*. The twenty-three-year-old Jacqueline Bisset had only a few small film roles to her credit when she appeared in *The Detective*, but her star was on the rise, and she appeared later that same year alongside Steve McQueen in *Bullitt*. Lee Remick was the exception, an established star whose stark beauty and emotional range had earned her a Best Actress Academy-Award nomination for *Days of Wine and Roses* (1962).

Although Bisset acquits herself nicely in a supporting role, Sinatra had planned on a different costar for *The Detective*. His wife at the time, Mia Farrow, had originally agreed to play the role of Norma MacIver, but when shooting began in October 1967, she was still working on *Rosemary's Baby* in California and production on that feature was run-ning over schedule. Sinatra was adamant that she leave her film. When she refused to join him in New York City for *The Detective* he considered it a betrayal. The following month, Sinatra had his lawyer serve Farrow with divorce papers right on the set of *Rosemary's Baby*. The marriage, which had lasted less than a year and a half, had been strained from the start, in large part because of the thirty-year age difference, and their choices in the next two months seemed to emphasize the generational gulf between them: Sinatra recorded an album of standards with Duke Ellington, and Farrow went to India with the Beatles to study transcen-dental meditation with the Maharishi Mahesh Yogi.

When *The Detective* opened in May 1968, the film's bold treatment of provocative subject matter and Sinatra's believable performance

"Some life I gave you. Out all day on the chase. And I bring it all home to you. Yeah, you got some deal, you did."

Joe Leland to Karen Wagner Leland

Opposite top: Joe at an impromptu police station press conference.

Opposite center: Joe studies a sketch of their main suspect along with (from left) Robbie (Al Freeman, Jr.), Schoenstein (Jack Klugman), and Nestor.

Opposite bottom: Schoenstein is Joe's one true ally on the force.

Top: Curran (Ralph Meeker) lets Joe know there's a bribe waiting for him if he drops the MacIver case.

Bottom: Sinatra with Jacqueline Bisset, who replaced Mia Farrow in the role of Norma.

mostly impressed critics. "The lurid plot line," wrote Hollis Alpert in *Saturday Review*, "is boldly enlivened by dialogue that still seems new to the recently liberalized screen. . . . Sinatra emerges as a solid actor as well as a solid citizen." Ray Loynd, in the *Hollywood Reporter*, called it Sinatra's best performance since *The Manchurian Candidate*, noting that he had "honed his laconic, hep veneer to the point of maximum credibility." Audiences also responded favorably to the film, making it one of the top-grossing movies of the year. The box office might have been even better if Sinatra's film had not been competing with that summer's cinema sensation, *Rosemary's Baby*, which opened two weeks after *The Detective*.

Viewed today, *The Detective* may strike some viewers as downright offensive in its stereotypical depiction of homosexuality. Yet in 1968, it was considered groundbreaking for a major studio release to portray gay life with at least some semblance of realism, if not nuance. To the filmmakers and Sinatra's credit, the title character displays glimmers of compassion for the gay men rounded up and abused by Duvall's Nestor; Leland also does not minimize or ignore how his actions played a role in an innocent man's execution. He may be cynical, but Leland hasn't jettisoned his conscience or his compassion. With immense subtlety, Sinatra reveals the emotions roiling beneath his character's worldly wise façade.

When it came to selecting dramatic roles, Sinatra wasn't content with material that was easy, or easily forgotten. He was aware that *The Detective* would shock and offend some moviegoers and even disappoint his faint-of-heart fans. But he also understood that it would appeal to audiences seeking riskier, adult-themed films. Cheerful escapist fare is often forgotten, but a dark, uncompromising film like *The Detective* lingers in the memory.

LADY IN CEMENT

A TWENTIETH CENTURY-FOX RELEASE | 1968

Director
Gordon Douglas

Screenplay
Marvin H. Albert and Jack Guss
Based on the novel by Albert

Principal Cast
Frank Sinatra (Tony Rome),
Raquel Welch (Kit Forrest),
Richard Conte (Lt. Dave Santini),
Dan Blocker (Waldo Gronsky),
Martin Gabel (Al Mungar),
Lainie Kazan (Maria Baretto), Pat
Henry (Rubin)

DONNING HIS trademark fedora, Sinatra returned to Miami for *Lady in Cement*, the genre-blurring sequel to *Tony Rome* (1967). More of a comedy-drama than its predecessor, Sinatra's fourth film with director Gordon Douglas brims with one-liners and sight gags. The tonal shift adds a winning dimension to a project that might otherwise have been a rehash, and refreshes a character who could have easily veered toward the pathetic. The comedy spin puts a cheerful glow on the life of the lowly Miami private eye, whose low-rent bachelor lifestyle and gambling addiction come off as little more than appealing character quirks. Sinatra's remarkable intuition about movies and his audience made it possible; if he changed things up to keep it interesting for himself, he knew the audience would find it interesting as well.

Exciting set pieces ensure that *Lady in Cement*, with all its levity, still packs a punch. The best of those scenes opens the picture, with Rome scuba diving off the southern Florida coast in search of sunken treasure and instead finding a dead woman on the ocean floor, her feet encased in cement. On the way back to the surface, he must navigate his way through a group of predator sharks, and he slaps them around with the same lack of concern he uses when roughing up hoodlums on dry land. Soon it's Rome who's getting knocked around though.

> ## "C'mon, let's hoist the martini flag."

Tony Rome (Sinatra) to Rubin (Pat Henry)

Tony Rome alerts the Coast Guard that he's just discovered a dead body off the Florida coast.

> ## "The law works for the law. Rome works for the money. That makes him easy to trust."

Waldo Gronsky (Dan Blocker) to Lt. Dave Santini (Richard Conte)

> ## "You been throwing me like a knuckleball. Too many people die around you."

Tony Rome to Waldo Gronsky

He's hired to find a missing woman by enormous ex-con Waldo Gronsky (Dan Blocker), a bruiser who greets Rome by throttling him and casually tossing him on the floor. As impulsive and violent as Gronsky is, Rome agrees to take on his case, which leads him next to the home of heiress Kit Forrest (Raquel Welch), a hard-drinking socialite who may know something about the murdered woman if only she could remember what she did last night. Her neighbor and protector is Al Mungar (Martin Gabel), a pint-sized mobster who would take Rome out in a second if he weren't concerned about his high blood pressure. More dead bodies turn up, and when his friend and brother-in-law, Lt. Dave Santini (Richard Conte), informs Rome that he's close enough to the crimes to be considered a suspect, he goes on the run, stealing Santini's car, then taking off on foot with Miami's finest in close pursuit. He knows he's being framed, so his freedom depends on his solving the case before he's reined in by the cops.

Lady in Cement continues the saga of the wayward Miami bachelor sleuth, at ease in every situation but most content in the grimy confines of his boat or enjoying a day at the track. But *Lady in Cement* is very different from *Tony Rome* because of the ramped-up humor, with Rome cracking wise and delivering great zingers that are punctuated with Sinatra's hilarious come-what-may shrugs and smirks. Especially effective is the dynamic between Rome and Blocker's Gronsky, as in the scene where one of their rough-and-tumble discussions ends with Rome being deposited on top of a bar, his legs dangling and eyes wide in amazement. The big guy vs. small guys jokes continue in *Lady in Cement,* with Gronsky smashing one interloper after another while the relatively tiny Sinatra scrambles to get out of the way, and gazes at his moose-like protector with appreciation and awe. Rome's quips with Lt. Santini are also comical, and the film ventures into the absurd in the extended chase scene when Santini and his squad pursue Rome through a luxury hotel where, among the sunbathing tourists, he is clearly out of place. The hotel itself is an inside joke; Sinatra was performing regularly at Miami's Fontainebleau, the location of the onscreen chase.

Opposite top: The excitable Waldo Gronsky (Dan Blocker) greets Rome with all the charm he can muster.

Opposite center: Adjusting his disguise, undercover cop Rubin (Pat Henry) tells Rome what he's heard about the ex-con Gronsky.

Opposite bottom: Rome meets the enigmatic Kit Forrest (Raquel Welch) poolside at her estate.

Above: Rome dives for his gun after being ambushed by goons.

Opposite top: On the search for clues, Rome visits his injured client Waldo Gronsky in the hospital.

Opposite center: Rome relaxes at the racetrack with Kit Forrest.

Opposite bottom: With Lt. Santini in pursuit, Rome crashes a seniors' dance at the Fontainebleau Hotel.

Raquel Welch is the only let down in the cast of *Lady in Cement*. A popular sex symbol at the time, she is featured in a variety of revealing outfits that showcase her beauty and poise, but her line readings lack comic timing and she has no chemistry with Sinatra. Though she's meant to be Rome's love interest in the film, he seems decidedly disinterested, and he conveys that apathy to the audience every time these two stars share the screen.

Lady in Cement fared well at the box office and reviews were positive, with critics focusing on the ways in which Sinatra and his team had improved upon the previous Tony Rome film. "The sequel to Sinatra's original Miami Beach lounge act is better," John Mahoney stated plainly in *The Hollywood Reporter* adding that, "It manages to have fun at its own expense." Charles Champlin in the *Los Angeles Times* praised Sinatra for creating a multi-dimensional character, a blend of "insouciance, cynicism, battered but surviving idealism, wisecrackery, courage, libido, thirst, and all the more interesting hungers." The film entertains, he added, because "He clearly enjoys the role . . ."

Lady in Cement is not Sinatra's most heralded picture, but it marked a high point in his career that film stars of any era would envy. He had long had the power to secure top-notch original material, A-list costars, and a production team of his choosing. For years, he had also had the clout to insist on a shooting schedule that fit with his almost-constant slate of live performances and recording sessions. What made the Tony Rome films exceptional was the fact that he now had a character that was a perfect fit as well. Like the savvy sleuth he played, Sinatra really had been around and seen a lot, and landed exactly where he wanted to be. He may have been unwilling to make that declaration in the press, but he wasn't afraid to say it in song. Shortly after *Lady in Cement* opened, he walked into a recording studio and laid down the track for his signature song, "My Way."

DIRTY DINGUS MAGEE

AN MGM RELEASE | 1970

Director
Burt Kennedy

Screenplay
Tom Waldman, Frank Waldman,
and Joseph Heller

Based on the novel *The Ballad
of Dingus Magee* by David
Markson

Principal Cast
Frank Sinatra (Dingus Magee),
George Kennedy (Hoke Birdsill),
Anne Jackson (Belle Knops),
Lois Nettleton (Prudence Frost),
Jack Elam (John Wesley
Hardin), Michele Carey (Anna
Hot Water), John Dehner
(Brigadier General George)

AN EMBARRASSINGLY sophomoric parody of western films aimed squarely at the lowest common denominator, *Dirty Dingus Magee* is one of Sinatra's worst films, right up there with *The Kissing Bandit* (1948). Playing the title role in an ill-fitting toupee, Sinatra at least seems to be enjoying himself in this labored, broad comedy, which has none of the satiric bite of its source material, David Markson's critically lauded novel, *The Ballad of Dingus Magee*.

Produced and directed by Burt Kennedy, who had scored a modest hit with the genial western comedy *Support Your Local Sherriff!* (1969), *Dirty Dingus Magee* turns Markson's nineteen-year-old protagonist into a grizzled, middle-aged Lothario—"the most unwanted outlaw in the West." When he's not bedding down with the nubile Native-American babe Anna Hot Water (Michele Carey), Dingus enjoys nothing more than playing an escalating game of one-upmanship with his dimwitted rival, Hoke Birdsill (George Kennedy). Robbed by Magee for the umpteenth time, Birdsill turns to madam Belle Knops (Anne Jackson), the mayor of Yerkes Hole, New Mexico, for help. She promptly appoints Birdsill sherriff—a decision she'll later reverse by giving the job to Magee. While Magee and Birdsill play out their long-running feud in a series of cartoonish set pieces, *Dirty Dingus Magee* drags to its conclusion.

> "Well, I'll be, the whole goddamned army is looking for me. Me, Dingus Magee!"

Dirty Dingus Magee (Sinatra)

> "Sometime I wish I wasn't so damned rotten."

Dirty Dingus Magee

> "His squaw called him the hottest pistol in the West."

Dirty Dingus Magee trailer

Left: Sinatra as the title character—originally a nineteen-year-old outlaw in David Markson's novel.

Right: Dingus gets the drop on his rival, Hoke Birdsill (George Kennedy).

When it was published in 1964, Markson's novel was hailed by *Life* magazine as "the most genuinely, unabashedly comic novel to come out in many a gloomy season." There was potential for a great film, yet the result, cowritten by slumming *Catch-22* author Joseph Heller, resembles nothing more than a racy episode of the 1960s–era sitcom *F-Troop*. Although Sinatra had certainly made his share of clunkers since the days of *From Here to Eternity* (1953), *Dirty Dingus Magee* marked a new low for the star. Critics were nearly unanimous in their scorn for Sinatra's first film in two years; Roger Greenspun of the *New York Times* pronounced *Dirty Dingus Magee* "dreadful." So how did Sinatra wind up in this dud?

The mostly widely accepted explanation is that the star was looking for a distraction from grieving the loss of his father, who had died of heart disease in 1969. The bawdy slapstick of *Dirty Dingus Magee* was just the tonic Sinatra needed to assuage his loss. Unfortunately, whatever relief he may have derived from playing the rowdy title character did not compensate for the ineptitude of the filmmaking. A box-office flop, *Dirty Dingus Magee* brought Sinatra's film career to a temporary halt; ten years would pass before he took another role in a feature film.

Magee and Anna Hot Water (Michele Carey) clean up another mess in *Dirty Dingus Magee.*

THE FIRST DEADLY SIN

A FILMWAYS PICTURES, INC. RELEASE | 1980

Director
Brian G. Hutton

Screenplay
Mann Rubin

Based on the book by Lawrence
Sanders

Principal Cast
Frank Sinatra (Sgt. Edward X.
Delaney), Faye Dunaway
(Barbara Delaney), David Dukes
(Daniel Blank), James Whitmore
(Dr. Sanford Ferguson), Martin
Gabel (Christopher Langley),
Brenda Vaccaro (Monica Gilbert)

THE FIRST DEADLY SIN marked both Sinatra's comeback after a ten-year absence from film, and the last film he would make. Based on Lawrence Sanders' popular series of crime-detective novels, Brian G. Hutton's film was intended to be the start of a film franchise. Despite a few warm critical reviews, however, the film failed to thrill at the box office and Sinatra, who served as one of the film's executive producers, turned his energies back to his recording career.

The First Deadly Sin chronicles the personal and professional pressures of Sgt. Edward X. Delaney (Sinatra), a by-the-book New York City cop *this close* to retirement. Any plans he may have had to retire peaceably, however, are soon shattered. His critically ill wife, Barbara (Faye Dunaway), undergoes emergency surgery on the same night that an ax-wielding serial killer strikes, leaving a man dead in the street. Whether because Delaney feels duty bound to protect the city, or because he's suffering some misplaced guilt for his wife's illness, Delaney refuses to go "gently into that good night" and instead pursues the killer, flouting precinct policy and the wishes of his superiors. He enlists help to track the killer from Monica Gilbert (Brenda Vaccaro), a victim's widow; Christopher Langley (Martin Gabel), a kindly if eccentric curator of arms and armor; and Dr. Sanford Ferguson (James Whitmore), a world-weary, wisecracking coroner.

"Yeah, that's pretty obvious."

Sgt. Delaney (Sinatra), in response to his wife's doctor admitting he's not God

"Nothing's safe."

Sgt. Delaney

"She's my whole world!"

Sgt. Delaney, referring to his wife.

Left: Sinatra as Edward Delaney, a by-the-book police sergeant on the trail of a serial killer.

Right: Academy Award winner Faye Dunaway costarred as Delaney's critically ill wife, Barbara.

Set in a modern New York City, *Deadly Sin* manages to re-create the look and feel of classic Hollywood noir: The city streets are dark and desolate; steam rises out of manholes; even the Christmas lights marking the season feel cold and jarring. Director Hutton and cinematographer Jack Priestly also throw in some striking visual touches that attempt to connect Delaney's personal dilemmas with the social. Even Delaney himself, from his wardrobe to his wry banter, seems to have stepped straight out of a 1940s gumshoe drama. But the stark existentialism of 1940s noir is here traded for a kind of reluctant resignation. Sinatra is not the obsessive, tortured personality we might expect to find (he doesn't even appear to drink on the sly). As Roger Ebert notes in his review, he is simply "dogged." Even Vaccaro's character Monica asks, "What hardworking person in this city *doesn't* have enemies?" with a quiet matter-of-factness. Both Delaney and Monica strike the viewer as people who clearly aren't happy about the way things are, but have long since accepted them with a grim determination.

While the procedural elements now feel dated (anyone who has watched episodic television in the last twenty years will know what to expect), and the hospital drama becomes a plot-stopper, director Hutton and writer Mann Rubin (who won an Edgar Allen Poe Award for Best Motion Picture), as well as Sinatra himself, crafted a grounded, sympathetic hero. We never glean much about Sinatra's and Dunaway's relationship, nor does her deteriorating state push the story forward, but the two obviously remain close and loving. While Dunaway gets little to do, her mature, charismatic sex appeal is an intelligent choice to pump blood into an otherwise passive role. But what viewers respond to in this film is, without doubt, Sinatra. He's allowed to be both tough and supremely vulnerable, revealing the cracks in his own armor without becoming maudlin or pitiable.

Columbia Pictures had originally hired Roman Polanski to direct, but dropped him when a well-known scandal erupted around him involving charges of statutory rape. One wonders what the film might have been had Polanski remained in the director's chair. As Ebert notes,

Opposite top: Sergeant Delaney appears to suffer a crisis of faith as he returns to the scene of the first murder.

Opposite bottom: The opening shots capture the look and feel of classic film noir.

Top: James Whitmore provides some much-needed comic relief as Dr. Ferguson, the medical examiner.

Center: Cinematographer Jack Priestley captures the chiaroscuro look of 1940s noir in *The First Deadly Sin*.

Bottom: Brenda Vaccaro as Monica Gilbert, the widow of the killer's first victim.

The First Deadly Sin doesn't play by its own rules. The killer (David Dukes) is revealed early on, but only in glimpses, and only when the filmmakers feel like it. Also, the filmmakers apparently found themselves in a quandary over Dukes' casting. At the time, he was appearing on Broadway in *Bent,* as a prisoner in a concentration camp. With his hair closely shorn for the role, he didn't fully look the part of the upper-class killer necessary for *The First Deadly Sin,* so he was given a toupee, which noticeably fails to cooperate in a few scenes. The filmmakers attempted to work around this by giving their killer a dual identity of sorts, but it's an identity crisis that is never given its narrative due.

Despite its shortcomings, *The First Deadly Sin* is perhaps more noteworthy than popular or critical reactions might suggest. It seems to exist on a critical pendulum swing between nostalgia and progress, between the old and new Hollywood. Released in 1980, it followed in the wake of everything from the youth movement, the sexual revolution, and Vietnam to Watergate and disco. It at once captures a contemporary sentiment that nothing is safe or sacred anymore as the old order had been upended, while also maintaining a very "retro" need to cling to what perhaps should remain sacred.

The killer on the hunt.

Stylistically, the film had the unenviable task of competing with Hollywood's young upstarts such as George Lucas, Steven Spielberg, and Martin Scorsese. While Lucas and Spielberg were reinventing classic Hollywood cinema as post-modern, high-adrenaline popcorn fare, and Scorsese was pushing the limits of "outsider" cinema with a candid, visceral style, *Deadly Sin* feels very much like old Hollywood. It's the kind of film Sinatra may have been drawn to back in his heyday. Perhaps he viewed it as a chance to introduce a new generation of filmgoers to Hollywood's, and his own, golden era. If that is the case, the film is a rare gift. Sinatra is that tough-guy film hero passing his fedora on to the next generation. For fans of Sinatra, *The First Deadly Sin* is therefore worth revisiting as the Chairman of the Board's cinematic swan song.

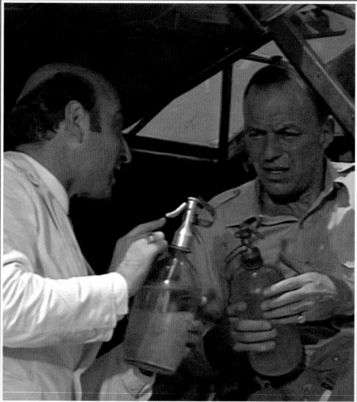

Left: Sinatra in *That's Entertainment*.

Right: Sinatra in *Cast a Giant Shadow*.

OTHER SINATRA FILMS
1965–1991

THE OSCAR
A PARAMOUNT PICTURES RELEASE · 1966

DIRECTOR	Russell Rouse
SCREENPLAY	Harlan Ellison, Clarence Greene, and Russell Rouse
	Based on the novel by Richard Sale
PRINCIPAL CAST	Stephen Boyd (Frankie Fane), Elke Sommer (Kay Bergdahl), Milton Berle (Kappy Kapstetter), Eleanor Parker (Sophie Cantaro), Joseph Cotten (Kenneth Regan), Jill St. John (Laurel Scott), Tony Bennett (Hymie Kelly), Edie Adams (Trina Yale), Ernest Borgnine (Barney Yale)

A camp classic relished by bad movie lovers, *The Oscar* is a cliché-ridden showbiz saga about the rise and fall of amoral movie star Frankie Fane (Stephen Boyd). Playing himself, Sinatra appears in the film's closing scene at the Academy Awards ceremony, where he wins the Best Actor statuette coveted by Fane.

CAST A GIANT SHADOW
A UNITED ARTISTS RELEASE · 1966

DIRECTOR	Melville Shavelson
SCREENPLAY	Melville Shavelson
	Based on the book by Ted Berkman
PRINCIPAL CAST	Kirk Douglas (Mickey Marcus), Senta Berger (Magda Simon), Angie Dickinson (Emma Marcus), James Donald (Safir), Stathis Giallelis (Ram Oren), Luther Adler (Jacob Zion), Gary Merrill (Pentagon Chief of Staff), Topol (Abou Ibn Kader), Frank Sinatra (Vince), Yul Brynner (Asher), John Wayne (General Randolph)

In this ambitious but uneven period drama about the founding of Israel, Sinatra plays a devil-may-care pilot hired by the Israeli army to fight their Arab enemies. Unfortunately, the Israelis are too broke to provide him with real ammunition, so he lobs seltzer bottles from the cockpit to unnerve the enemy; the bottles supposedly make a screaming sound when dropped from above.

THAT'S ENTERTAINMENT!
AN MGM RELEASE · 1974

DIRECTOR	Jack Haley, Jr.
SCREENPLAY	Jack Haley, Jr.
PRINCIPAL CAST	Fred Astaire, Bing Crosby, Gene Kelly, Peter Lawford, Liza Minnelli, Donald O'Connor, Debbie Reynolds, Mickey Rooney, Frank Sinatra, James Stewart, Elizabeth Taylor

Sinatra joins fellow luminaries from the golden age of MGM musicals, including former costars Bing Crosby and Gene Kelly, to introduce dazzling clips from the studio vault. Among the highlights are the opening number from *On the Town* (1949) and Sinatra's duet with Crosby in *High Society* (1956).

CANNONBALL RUN II
A WARNER BROS. RELEASE · **1984**

DIRECTOR | Hal Needham

SCREENPLAY | Harvey Miller, Hal Needham, and Albert S. Ruddy

PRINCIPAL CAST | Burt Reynolds (J. J. McClure), Dom DeLuise (Victor Prinzim/Captain Chaos), Dean Martin (Jamie Blake), Sammy Davis, Jr. (Fenderbaum), Jamie Farr (The Sheik), Marilu Henner (Betty), Telly Savalas (Hymie), Shirley MacLaine (Veronica)

Sinatra reunited with his Rat Pack pals to make a cameo appearance as himself in this abysmal sequel to the 1981 blockbuster about a cross-country road race. He at least maintains some semblance of dignity, which is more than can be said for his costars.

LISTEN UP! THE LIVES OF QUINCY JONES
A WARNER BROS. RELEASE · **1991**

DIRECTOR | Ellen Weissbrod

SCREENPLAY | Ellen Weissbrod

PRINCIPAL CAST | Ray Charles, Miles Davis, Billy Eckstine, Ella Fitzgerald, Flavor Flav, Dizzy Gillespie, Alex Haley, Herbie Hancock, Ice-T, Michael Jackson, Big Daddy Kane, Sidney Lumet, Bobby McFerrin, Frank Sinatra, Steven Spielberg, Barbra Streisand, Oprah Winfrey

Sinatra appears briefly in this documentary to pay tribute to the talents of the celebrated composer and music producer, who had worked with Sinatra at the Sands in the 1960s.

BIBLIOGRAPHY

Academy of Motion Picture Arts and Sciences. Academy of Motion Picture Arts and Sciences. www.oscars.org.

AllMusic. Rovi Corporation. www.allmusic.com.

All About Jazz. AllAboutJazz. www.allaboutjazz.com.

American Ballet Theatre. American Ballet Theatre. www.abt.org.

Barnes, Ken. Commentary. *The Man with the Golden Arm* 50th Anniversary Edition DVD. Hart Sharp Video, 2005.

Biography.com. A&E Television Networks. www.biography.com.

Crazy For Cinema. Crazy For Cinema. www.crazy4cinema.com.

Curtis, Tony. Photographs, *Sergeants 3. Ebony*, April 1962.

DVD Talk. DVDTalk.com. www.dvdtalk.com.

Filmsite. American Movie Classics Company LLC. www.filmsite.org.

Freedland, Michael. *All the Way: A Biography of Frank Sinatra.* New York: St. Martin's Press, 1997.

Harris, Mark. *Pictures at a Revolution: Five Movies and the Birth of the New Hollywood.* New York: The Penguin Press HC, 2008.

Havers, Richard. *Sinatra.* London: Dorling Kindersley Limited, 2004.

Hirsch, Foster. *Otto Preminger: The Man Who Would be King.* New York: Alfred A. Knopf, 2007.

Hollywood Foreign Press Association. Hollywood Foreign Press Association.

www.goldenglobes.org

Howlett, John. *Frank Sinatra.* Philadelphia: Courage Books, 1980.

Jewell, Derek. *Frank Sinatra: A Celebration.* Boston: Little Brown, 1985.

Kelley, Kitty. *His Way: An Unauthorized Biography of Frank Sinatra.* New York: Bantam Books, 1986.

Levy, Shawn. *Rat Pack Confidential.* New York: Doubleday, 1988.

McNally, Karen. *When Frankie Went to Hollywood: Frank Sinatra and American Male Identity.*

Champaign, IL: University of Illinois Press, 2008.

New York Times. The New York Times Company. www.nytimes.com.

Petkov, Stephen and Leonard Mustazza (eds.). *The Frank Sinatra Reader.* New York: Oxford University Press USA, 1997.

Quirk, Lawrence J. and William Schoell. *The Rat Pack: Neon Nights with the King of Cool.* New York: Harper, 2003.

Reel.com. Hollywood Video Corporation. www.reel.com.

Ringgold, Gene and Clifford McCarty. *The Films of Frank Sinatra*. Secaucus, NJ: Carol Publishing Group, 1971, 1993.

Santopietro, Tom. *Sinatra in Hollywood*. New York: St. Martin's Press, 2008.

ShirleyMaclaine.com. ShirleyMacLaine.com, Inc. and MacLaine Enterprises, Inc.

www.shirleymaclaine.com.

Simmons, Jerold. "Challenging the Production Code: The Man with the Golden Arm." *Journal of Popular Film & Television*. Washington: Spring 2005, Vol. 33, Iss. 1, pages 39–49.

Sinatra, Jr., Frank. Commentary. *Robin and the Seven Hoods* DVD. Warner Bros. Entertainment, Inc. 2005.

_____. Commentary. *Sergeants 3* DVD. United Artists, 2008.

Sinatra, Nancy. *Frank Sinatra: An American Legend*. Santa Monica, CA: General Publishing Group, 1995.

Summers, Anthony and Robbyn Swan. *Sinatra: The Life*. Alfred A. Knopf, 2005.

Time.com. Time Inc. www.time.com

Turner Classic Movies. Turner Classic Movies, a Time Warner Company. www.tcm.com.

Variety.com. Reed Business Information, a division of Reed Elsevier, Inc. www.variety.com.

Wayne, Jane Ellen. *The Leading Men of MGM*. New York: Carrol & Graf Publishers, 2004.

Wikipedia. The Wikimedia Foundation. www.wikipedia.org.

Williams, Esther and Digby Diehl. *The Million Dollar Mermaid*. New York: Simon & Schuster, 1999.

Zehme, Bill. *The Way You Wear Your Hat: Frank Sinatra and the Lost Art of Livin'*. New York: Harper Collins, 1997.

Zinnemann, Tim and Alvin Sargent. Commentary. *From Here to Eternity* DVD. Columbia TriStar Home Entertainment, 2001.

INDEX

NOTE: Page references in italics indicate illustrations and captions.

A

An Affair to Remember, 146

Albright, Lola, *119*

Alda, Robert, 114

Aldrich, Robert, 242, 245

Algren, Nelson, 124, 131

Allen, Woody, 238

All Fall Down, 230

All in the Family, 238

Allyson, June, 48

Alpert, Hollis, 117, 149, 292, 301

Altrock, Nick, 52

Anchors Aweigh, 20, 23, 28–35, 62

Andress, Ursula, *244–45*

Armstrong, Louis, 139, *141*

Arnold, Edward, 55, *56*

Around the World in Eighty Days, *188*, 189

Assault on a Queen (film), 260, 280–84

Assault on a Queen (novel; Finney), 280

Astaire, Fred, 199, *199*

Axelrod, George, 228

B

Bacall, Lauren, 84

Bakaleinikoff, Constantin, 18

Bakalyan, Richard, 264, *264–65*, *272–73*

Ball, Lucille, 230

The Ballad of Dingus Magee (Markson), 308, 310

Barbato, Nancy. *See* Sinatra, Nancy Barbato

Barefoot in the Park (stage play), 238

Baretta, 291

Barnes, Howard, 24, 26

Barry, Philip, 140

Barrymore, Ethel, *103*

Bathing Beauty, *50*

Beatles, The, 253, 299

Bell, Thalia, 35

Benedek, Lázló, 46

Berkeley, Busby, 48, 51

Bernstein, Leonard, 58

Bewitched, *215*

The Bible . . . In the Beginning, 272

The Big Broadcast, 18

The Big Sleep, 291

The Big Street, 230

Bill, Tony, *237*

Billboard, 106

Biroc, Joseph, *218*

Bishop, Joey, 84, 191, 205

Bisset, Jacqueline, 299, *300*

Blackmer, Sidney, *142–43*

Blaine, Vivian, *113*, 114, *116*

The Blob, 182

Blocker, Dan, *304–7*, 305

Bodeen, Dewitt, 43

Bogart, Humphrey, 84, 158, 291–92

Boretz, Allen, 23

Borgnine, Ernest, *90–91*

The Boston Strangler, 294

Boucher, Anthony, 284

Brando, Marlon, 114, *115–16*, 117, 124

The Bridge on the River Kwai, 212

Britton, Pamela, 30

Brolin, James, *272–73*

Bronson, Charles, *184–85*, 185

Brooks, Mel, 238

Brown, Edmund, 287

Brown, Harry, 205

Bullitt, 275

Buono, Victor, *244–45*

Burnett, W. R., 223

Burr, Raymond, 74, *76*

C

Caesar's Hour, 238

Cahn, Sammy, 24, 28, 36, 150, 179, 246, 253

Caine, Michael, 287

Can-Can (film), 194–201

Can-Can (stage musical), 196

Cannonball Run II, 260n, 276, 321

Cantinflas, 255

Capitol Records, 84, 192

Capra, Frank, 174, 176

Carey, Michele, *311*

Carmen Jones, 126

Cast a Giant Shadow, *318*, 320

Catto, Max, 212

Chamales, Tom T., 180

Champlin, Charles, 306

Chevalier, Maurice, 195, 196, 197

The Children's Hour, 223

Chitty Chitty Bang Bang, 294

Cinema (book), 245

Clifford, Frank, 284, 287

Clift, Montgomery, 87, 88, *91*, 92, 108

Coal Miner's Daughter, 153

Cobb, Lee J., *237*

Cohn, Harry, 88, 91–92, 129, 156

The Colgate Comedy Hour, 238

The Collector, 287

Collins, Joan, *257*

Comden, Betty, 58, 62

Come Blow Your Horn (film), 236–41

Come Blow Your Horn (stage play), 238

Come Fly with Me, 166

Condon, Richard, 228, 230

Conte, Richard, *291*, 292

Contract on Cherry Street, 260

Cook, Willis, *215*

Corliss, Richard, 192

Count Basie, 80, 192

Coward, Noel, 84

Crain, Jeane, *152–53*

Crawford, Broderick, 110

Crawford, Joan, 245

Crosby, Bing, 11, 14, 18, 39, 55, 136, *137*, 139, *141–42*, 192, *252–53*, 253, *257*, 320

Crowther, Bosley, 18, 26, 51, 55, 62, 94, 110, 131, 136, 139–40, 172, 179, 187, 196, 233, 245, 267, 283, 292

Curtis, Tony, *163–65*, *167*, 223, 227

D

Dark, Christopher, *97*

Davis, Bette, 245

Davis, Sammy, Jr., 84, 185, 191, *204*, 205, *206*, *222*, *247*, 248, *250–52*, 253

Davison, Davey, *278–79*

Day, Doris, 100, *102*, *104–5*, 105–6

Days of Wine and Roses, 299

Death Wish, 260

DeHaven, Gloria, *22–27*, 24

de Havilland, Olivia, *110–11*

The Detective (film), 260, 294–301

The Detective (novel; Thorp), 294

The Devil at 4 O'Clock, 212–19

Dexter, Brad, *264–65*

Dickinson, Angie, 205, *209*

DiMaggio, Joe, 158

Dirty Dingus Magee, 260, 308–11

Dirty Harry, 260

Donaldson, Harold, 16

Donen, Stanley, 46, 48, 51, 58, 62

Donohue, Jack, 280, 283, *283*

Dorsey, Jimmy, 134

Dorsey, Tommy, 13, 134

Double Dynamite, 66–73

Douglas, Gordon, 100, 248, 302

Down Beat, 14

Duke, Patty, 233

Dukes, David, 317

Dunaway, Faye, *313*, 315

Durante, Jimmy, 36, *38–39*

Duvall, Robert, *295*, 299

E

Eastwood, Clint, 264

Ebert, Roger, 315, 317

Edens, Roger, 62

The Ed Sullivan Show, 84

Ekberg, Anita, *244–45*

Ellington, Duke, 80, 192, 283

Errol, Leon, 16

Essex, 156

F

Falk, Peter, *249*, 253

Fapp, Daniel L., 165–66

Farrow, John, 275

Farrow, Mia, 192, 259, *261*, 272, 275, 279, 287, 299

Finney, Jack, 280

The First Deadly Sin, 260, 312–17

Flynn, Hazel, 227

Ford, John, 223

Four Daughters, 100

4 for Texas, 242–45

Franciosa, Anthony, 283

Frankenheimer, John, 192, 228, 230, 233

The Frank Sinatra Show, 158

Frank Sinatra Sings for Only the Lonely, 166

Fraser, Elisabeth, *102*

Freed, Arthur, 62

Freeman, Al, Jr., *298–99*

Frees, Paul, *97*

The French Connection, 275

From Here to Eternity (film), 11, 20, 83–84, 86–93

From Here to Eternity (novel; Jones), 83, 86

Furie, Sidney J., 284, 287

G

Gardner, Ava, 14, 61, 69, 71, 84, *85*, 91–92, 146, 149, 272, 275

Garland, Judy, 48, 51, 84

Garrett, Betty, 51, *53*, 55, *60–61*, 61, *63–65*

Gates, Nancy, 98, *98*

Gaynor, Mitzi, *151*

Giancana, Sam, 172, 192

Gigi, 172

Gilda, 153, 158

Gillmore, Margalo, *142–43*

Gleason, James, *97*

The Godfather, 260

The Gold of Naples, 146

Goodman, Benny, 23

Grahame, Gloria, *37*

Grant, Cary, *145*, 146, *147*, *148*

Grayson, Kathryn, 30, *34*, 36, *37*, 44, *45*, *46–47*

The Great St. Louis Bank Robbery, 182, 185

Green, Alolph, 58, 62

Greenberg, Abe, 275

Greenspun, Roger, 310

Gregory, James, *230–31*

Gunga Din (Kipling), 223

The Guns of Navarone, 212

Guys and Dolls (film), 112–17, 124

Guys and Dolls (stage musical), 112, 114

H

Hamilton, Sara, 39

A Hard Day's Night, 253

Harding, John Briard, 44, 46

Hart, Lorenz, 16, 158

Harvey, Laurence, *232*, *234*

Hayden, Sterling, 98

Hayworth, Rita, 154, *156–58*, 158, *160*

Hecht, Ben, 43

Heller, Joseph, 310

Henderson, Douglas, *229*

Henreid, Paul, *184–85*

Henry, Pat, *304–5*

Hepburn, Katharine, 136, 140

Higher and Higher, 16–20

High Noon, 88

High Society, 18, 136–43, 320

Hoch, Winton C., 223

Hodges, Eddie, *175*, *177*, 179

A Hole in the Head, 174–79

Holm, Celeste, *121–22*, *138–39*, 139

Hope, Bob, 55, *257*

The House I Live In, 80, 166

House Un-American Activities Committee, 14

Howard, Trevor, *271–73*, *274–75*

Hughes, Howard, 71

Huston, John, 256

Hutton, Brian G., 312, 315

Hyer, Martha, *169*, 172, *172*

I

I Love Lucy, 230

In the Wee Small Hours, 84, 105

It Happened in Brooklyn, 36–39

It Happened One Night, 174

It's a Wonderful Life, 174

Iturbi, José, 30, *34–35*

J

The Jack Benny Program, 238

Jackson, Sammy, *264–65*

James, Harry, 23

Janney, Russell, 40

Jewell, Derek, 191

Johnny Concho, 132–35

Johnson, Richard, *183–85*

The Joker Is Wild, 150–53

Jones, Carolyn, *175*, *177*, 179

Jones, Dean, 185

Jones, James, 83, 86, 168

Jones, Quincy, 321

Jourdan, Louis, 196, *198–99*, 199

K

Kael, Pauline, 233, 287

Kato, Takeshi, *266–67*

Kaye, Stubby, 114, *116*

Keawe, George, 267

Keith, Robert, *102*

Kelly, Gene, 11, 14, *15*, 23, 28, *29–31*, 30, 32, *34*, 35, 48, *49*, *50–51*, 51–52, 58, *59–60*, 60–62, *63–64*, 154, 320

Kelly, Grace, 136, *137–39*, 139, *141–43*

Kennedy, Arthur, *170–71*, 172

Kennedy, Burt, 308

Kennedy, George, *309*

Kennedy, John F., 94, 179, 191–92, 205, 218, 228, 230, 233, 235, 248

Kennedy, Robert, 191–92

Kerr, Deborah, *88–89*, 91, 276, *277–79*, 279

Khrushchev, Nikita, 199

Kings Go Forth, 162–67

Kingsley, Dorothy, 156, 196

Kipling, Rudyard, 223

Kirk, Phyllis, *133*

The Kissing Bandit, 14, 40, 44–47

Klugman, Jack, *298–99*, 299

Koch, Howard W., 264

Kohlmar, Fred, 156

Komack, Jimmy, *177*

Kramer, Stanley, 108, 110, 144, 149

Krim, Arthur, 228, 230

Kubrick, Stanley, 228

L

Lady in Cement, 302–7

Lamour, Dorothy, 55

Lancaster, Burt, *88–89*, 91, *91*

Lang, Charles, 105

Lang, Walter, 194, 199

Lansbury, Angela, 230, *230–32*, 233, *234*

Las Vegas Nights, 13, 20, 79

Laughton, Charles, 228

Laura, 126

Lawford, Peter, 36, *37*, 84, 185, 191, *204*, 205, *206*, *221*

Lear, Norman, 236, 238, 241

Le Carré, John, 284

Lederer, Charles, 196, 205

Leigh, Janet, *230*

Lennart, Isobel, 44, 46, 189

LeRoy, Mervyn, 80, 212, 216

Lester, Buddy, 205, *222*

Letters from Iwo Jima, 264

Levy, Shawn, 227

Lewis, Jerry, 171

Lewis, Joe E., 150

Lisi, Virna, 280, *281*, 283

Listen Up!: The Lives of Quincy Jones, 260n, 321

The List of Adrian Messenger, 256

Loesser, Frank, 112, 114

Lollobrigida, Gina, *181*, 185, 187

Loren, Sophia, *145*, 146, *147*, *148*

The Love Bug, 185

Love Me or Leave Me, 153

Loynd, Ray, 301

Luna, Barbara, *214*

Lund, John, *137, 139*

Lyon, Sue, *290–91*

M

MacLaine, Shirley, *169–71*, 172, *173*, *195–96*, 196, *197–99*, 199, *209*, 223

MacMurray, Fred, 40, *41*, 43

Mahesh Yogi, Maharishi, 299

Mahoney, John, 307

Malone, Dorothy, *102*

The Maltese Falcon, 291

Maltz, Albert, 191

A Man and His Music, 259

The Manchurian Candidate (film), 11, 192, 228–35

The Manchurian Candidate (novel; Condon), 228, 230

Mankiewicz, Joseph L., 117

Mann, Abby, 294

Mann, Stanley, 287

Manne, Shelley, 131

Manners, Dorothy, 166

The Man with the Golden Arm, 11, 83–84, 124–31, 228

Markson, David, 308, 310

Marriage on the Rocks, 260, 276–79, 283

Martin, Dean, 84, *170–71*, 171–72, *173*, 191, *204*, 205, *206*, *209*, *221*, 223, 242, *243–45*, 245, 248, *249*, *251–52*, 256, *257*, 276, *277*

Marvin, Lee, *110–11*

Marx, Groucho, *67–71*, 69, 72, *73*

Marx, Zeppo, 260

Marx Brothers, 23

Matray, Ernst, 24

Maude, 238

Maxwell, Marilyn, 36

Mayer, Louis B., 58, 71, 140

Mazurki, Mike, *244–45*

MCA, 14

McClay, Howard, 72

McGavin, Darren, *126*, 129

McGuire, Don, 74, 132

McGuire, Marcy, *17*

McGuire, Phyllis, *237*

McHugh, Jimmy, 16

McQueen, Steve, 182, *183*, 185

Medved, Harry and Michael, 40

Meeker, Ralph, *300*

Meet Danny Wilson, 71, 74–77

Meet Me in Las Vegas, 189

Melcher, Martin, 105

Menjou, Adolphe, 20, 23

MGM, 16, 28, 71

Mihashi, Tatsuya, 264

Miller, Ann, *60–61*, 61, 80

Milne, Tom, 110

Minnelli, Vincente, 171–72

The Miracle of the Bells, 40–43

The Miracle Worker, 233

Mitchum, Robert, 108, *109–11*, 110

Moffitt, Jack, 117

Monroe, Marilyn, 158

Morgan, Michèle, 16, *17–19*

Mortimer, Lee, 14

Mr. Smith Goes to Washington, 174

Mulhare, Edward, *274–75*

Munshin, Jules, *50–51*, 52, *59*, 61

Murphy, George, 20, *21*, 24

Murray, John, 23

N

Naish, J. Carrol, 44, *47*

The Naked Runner (film), 260, 284–87

The Naked Runner (novel; Clifford), 284, 287

Never So Few (film), 180–87

Never So Few (novel; Chamales), 180

Newman, Walter, 124

Newport, Michael, *286–87*

Nichol, Alex, 74, *76*, 77

The Night of the Hunter, 228

Niven, David, 84, 279

None But the Brave, 262–69

North by Northwest, 165

Not as a Stranger (film), 108–11

Not as a Stranger (novel; Thompson), 108

Novak, Kim, *125*, *127*, 129, *129*, 154, *155–56*, *158*, *160–61*

Nugent, Frank S., 23

Oakland, Simon, *293*

Ober, Philip, *87*

O'Brien, Liam, 212

Ocean's Eleven, 11, 172, 191, 202–11, 220

The Odd Couple, 299

The Odd Couple (stage play), 238

O'Hara, John, 156, 158

Okuda, Kikumaru, 264

Ol' Blue Eyes is Back, 260

Oliver! 294

On the Town, 11, 23, 36, 40, 48, 58–65, 320

On the Waterfront, 114, 117, 124

The Oscar, 319

O'Sullivan, Maureen, 275

Oswald, Lee Harvey, 94, 235

Paiva, Nestor, 66, *70–71*

Palance, Jack, 83

Pal Joey (film), 11, 154–61, 199

Pal Joey (stage musical), 154

Pan, Hermes, *198–99*, 199

Paramount Pictures, 13

Parker, Eleanor, *127–28*, *178*

Parrish, Leslie, *234*

Parsons, Louella, 35, 117

Paths of Glory, 228

Patrick, John, 168

Pearce, Alice, *63*

Peck, Steven, *170*

Pepe, 255

Pevney, Joseph, 74

Peyton Place, 272

Phillips, Carmen, *173*

Pichel, Irving, 40

Picon, Molly, *237*

Pied Pipers, 13, 79

Polanski, Roman, 315

Porter, Cole, 136, 139, 194, 196, 199

Powell, Eleanor, 14

Powers, James, 253

Preminger, Otto, 11, 83–84, 124, 126, 129, 131

Presley, Elvis, 11, 84, 192

Previn, André, 46

The Pride and the Passion, 110, 144–49

Priestly, Jack, 315, *316*

Production Code, 83–84, 131, 156, 228, 294

Prowse, Juliet, 192, 196, *197*, 199

Pully, B. S., 114, *117*

Quirk, Lawrence J., 74

Quo Vadis, 212

Ragland, Rags, 39

Rasumny, Mikhail, 44

Rat Pack, 84, 172, 191, 205, 208, *210–11*, 220, 321. *See also* Bishop, Joey; Davis, Sammy, Jr.; Lawford, Peter; Martin, Dean

Ray, 153

Red Scare, 14

Reed, Donna, *90–91*, 91–92

Remick, Lee, *296–97*, 299

Reprise Records, 192

Requiem for a Dream, 131

Reveille with Beverly, 80

Reynolds, Debbie, *121–22*

Reynolds, Quentin, 43

Riddle, Nelson, 84, 105, 246

Ritter, Thelma, *177*, 179

RKO, 16, 43, 71

The Road to Hong Kong, 256, *257*

Robbins, Jerome, 58

Robin and the 7 Hoods, 190, 246–53

Robinson, Edward G., 176, *177*, 179

Robson, Mark, 267, 272

The Rockford Files, 291

Rodgers, Richard, 16, 158

Romero, Cesar, 205, *278–79*

Room Service, 23

Rosemary's Baby, 299, 301

Ross, Frank, 80, 166

Ross, Lillian, *141*

Rowlands, Gena, 292

Rubin, Mann, 315

Rush, Barbara, *237*

Russell, Jane, 66, *67*, 69, 71–72, *71–73*

S

Sanders, Lawrence, 312

Sands, Tommy, 264, *264–65*, 279

Saul, Oscar, 150

Schacht, Al, 52

Scheur, Philip K., 134, 187

Schickel, Richard, 192

Schoell, William, 74

Schwartz, David R., 246

September of My Years, 259

Sergeants 3, 134, 220–27

Serling, Rod, 283

Seven Brides for Seven Brothers, 156

Shane, 83

Shaw, Artie, 83

Sheekman, Arthur, 168

Sherman, Teddi, 242, 245

Ship Ahoy, 14, 20, 79

Show Boat, 81

Shulman, Max, 123

Sidney, George, 156

Siegel, Sol, 139, 171

Silva, Henry, *222*

Silver, Johnny, 114, *116*

Silvers, Phil, 39

Simmons, Jean, *115–16*

Simon, Neil, 236, 238, 241

Sinatra, Barbara Marx, 260

Sinatra, Frank, Jr., 14, 192, 223, 248

Sinatra, Nancy, 14, 44, 276, 279

Sinatra, Nancy Barbato, 14, 36, 69, 71

Sinatra, Tina, 14

Sinatra Enterprises, 264

Sinatra in Hollywood (Santopietro), 283

Sincap, 174

Singin' in the Rain, 62

Skelton, Red, 14

Some Came Running (film), 166, 168–73

Some Came Running (novel; Jones), 168

Songs For Young Lovers, 92, 105

Spiegel, Sam, 124

St. John, Jill, *237*, *240*, *289–91*, 291–92, *293*

Stalag 17, 126

Step Lively, 20–27

Stewart, James, 140

Stockwell, Dean, *29*, 30

Stoll, George, 35

A Streetcar Named Desire, 150

Studio One, 132

Sturges, John, 223, 224, 227

Styne, Jule, 24, 28, 36

Suddenly, 11, 94–99

Suguro, Homare, *266–67*

Sullivan, Ed, 84

Support Your Local Sheriff! 308

Susaki, Katsuya, 264

T

Take Me Out to the Ball Game, *15*, 23, 48–57, 62

Tamiroff, Akim, 205

Taradash, Daniel, 86

The Tender Trap (film), 118–23

That's Entertainment, 318, 320

This is Sinatra! 123

Thompson, Morton, 108

Thompson, Thomas, 275

Thomson, David, 11

Thorp, Roderick, 294

3 Godfathers, 212

Till the Clouds Roll By, 78, 81

Tinee, Mae, 49

To Catch a Thief, 146

Todd, Mike, 189

Tom and Jerry, 32, *34*

Tommy Dorsey Orchestra, 13, 23

Tony Rome, 260, 288–93, 305, 307

Tormé, Mel, *17*

The Towering Inferno, 218–19

Tracy, Spencer, 212, *213–14*, 216, 218

True Grit, 299

Twist, John, 264

United Artists, 235

Vaccaro, Brenda, *316*

Valli, Alida, 40, *42–43*, 43

Van Heusen, Jimmy, 150, 179, 246, 253

Variety, 94, 106, 110, 131, 149, 160, 172, 208, 218, 245, 267

Vera-Ellen, *59*, 61, *63–64*

Verdon, Gwen, 196

Verne, Jules, 189

Vidor, Charles, 153

Von Ryan's Express (film), 259, 267, 270–75

Von Ryan's Express (novel; Westheimer), 272, 275

Von Stroheim, Erich, 126

Walker, Clint, *264–65*

Wallach, Eli, 91–92

Walters, Charles, 136

Warner, Jack, 246

Warner Bros., 264

Watertown, 260

Wayne, David, *119*

Weiler, A. H., 160, 227

Welch, Raquel, *304–7*, 307

We're No Angels, 212

Westheimer, David, 272, 275

What Ever Happened to Baby Jane? 245

Whitmore, James, *316*

Whorf, Richard, 39

Wilder, Billy, 126

William Morris Agency, 84

Williams, Esther, 48, *50*, 51

Williams, Tennessee, 150

Wilson, Dooley, *18–19*

Winston, Archer, 26

Winters, Shelley, 74, *75–76*, 77

Wood, Natalie, *164*, *166–67*

Wynn, Keenan, 179

Yorkin, Bud, 236, 238, 241

Young, Gig, *102*

Young at Heart, 100–107

Your Show of Shows, 238

Zinneman, Fred, 83, 86, 88, 91–92

ACKNOWLEDGMENTS

I received invaluable advice and assistance from many people while working on this book. First and foremost, I am especially grateful to Les Krantz, my mentor and frequent collaborator, whose persistence and vision made *Sinatra: Hollywood His Way* possible. I am also indebted to Cindy De La Hoz, my astute editor at Running Press, for her meticulous attention to detail and unerring judgment. Thanks to designer Jason Kayser and photo editor Debbi Andrews for their exemplary work. Kudos to Janet W. Morris for her editorial assistance. Finally, my sincere thanks to Greg Jones and everyone else at Running Press for their support.

It was my great good fortune to work with a gifted team of writers on *Sinatra: Hollywood His Way*. I cannot thank them enough for their sterling contributions and prodigious work ethic. I tip my hat in gratitude to Ken Dubois, Pam Grady, Sheila Lane, Ross M. Levine, Debra Ott, and James Plath.